The

GOLDEN
TICKET

to Your **DREAM JOB**

The expert's guide to being in the
TOP 1% OF APPLICANTS

ED ANDREW

First published in Australia in 2020.

Copyright@ Ed Andrew 2020

ISBN: 978-0-6488210-0-7

www.edandrew.com

The only rule for life is to be kind, to yourself, and to others.

TABLE OF CONTENTS

Part 9: Case Study—Contracting

Part 10: Hard Questions Answered

Part 11: Securing Your Future

Acknowledgements

INTRODUCTION

The key to securing that Golden Ticket in job search is the twin pillars of preparation and information. In essence job search means research. To join the exclusive club of the top 1% of jobseekers you need to arm yourself with the best data that you can find.

The benefits for you are simple; you will have the upper hand when it comes to every step of your job search journey. Personally I think that you will not just be in the top 1% but quite probably the top 0.1% of all jobseekers. The knowledge and insights I share with you are based on 30 years of experience across the world.

Often the key to accessing information is through recruiters and here you will learn all of the tips and tricks to managing them and optimising your job search. All of us, whether we are CEO's, graduates, professionals, office workers or tradespeople will at some stage apply for a job, or many jobs. We will need the help of a recruiter to manage our search for either that dream role or for one which will lead us to it.

A bad experience with a recruiter can sabotage the chances of landing your dream job. It happens every day. However, when you understand how the system works, you can open doors to jobs you did not know exist and build relationships that will serve you throughout your career. It requires effort, research and accountability on your part. If you are ready for that challenge, then you are in the right place.

You can break down the art of landing a job, whether it is your dream job or a fill-in role, into three factors. *Employers want to know:*

- Why you love them and want to work for them?
- What value and benefit can you bring to them?
- What impact can you make?

They want to know if you have experienced and resolved some of the challenges they face in their business. If not, can you learn how to address these better than anyone else while being the best fit for the team? *The twin factors every employer looks for are relevance and suitability:*

- Relevance is whether you have the hard and soft skills needed for the job.
- Suitability is about how you will fit into the culture of the business and whether your needs and aspirations for the role will drive you to do your best.

There can be many pitfalls in your job search that you, the unwary jobseeker, can fall victim to but there is an army of skilled dedicated career recruiters who will support you on your career journey. When you discover them, they will work with you and provide honest feedback on your aspirations. The good ones are rare, so prepare to do some research and maybe dig harder than you thought.

While the recruitment process can be frustrating, there is a golden rule for jobseekers and managing the process:

"If they have not called you back, it is for a reason. They have either nothing to say or they don't want to give you bad news."

One thing I can guarantee is that if an employer wants to interview you, then you will hear from them.

I have advised 'C' Suite Executives and coached more than 15,000 jobseekers to secure jobs in over 30 countries. I have been an employer for most of my life, across the globe, and built eight figure companies. However, I still used recruiters myself at certain times and my experience with them is not that different to yours. Like you, both recruiters and employers have ghosted me during the interview process and my experience as an employer hiring recruiters has been mixed. But that is balanced with having met and hired some incredibly talented people, people just like you.

I have seen the recruitment process from all ends of the spectrum, as the employer, head hunter and jobseeker. One of the first lessons is how to manage your expectations and not become frustrated by the process. Regardless of the number of unsuccessful applications you make, you only need one offer, with an employer you respect, to change your perspective. This guide will help you apply only for the roles suited to you and to only work with recruiters who support you. Your goal is to secure a job and you may have different expectations of the process and the amount of support that you need. All the information you need is here and you can pick which parts resonate best with you.

I can promise you that this guide will arm you with confidence, information and the best steps to take.

You will discover:

- How to find the right recruiter and access the best jobs
- How to manage your expectations
- How to manage recruiters
- How to find jobs through your network
- How to apply for jobs directly
- How to write a killer resume
- How to answer the hardest interview questions

- How to manage multiple interviews and offers
- How to write an All Star LinkedIn profile and why
- How to be next in mind when recruiters find your ideal job
- How to take control of your career
- How to create a mission for your job search and plan your future

You will have all the tools to secure the job that best serves your needs. This includes making sure that technology works for you, such as creating your LinkedIn profile, enabling recruiters to find you even when you are on the beach, up a mountain or sleeping. A common question is how to manage approaches from recruiters and I discuss that topic with practical solutions.

I walk you through examples of scenarios and suggest the do's and do not's, what to expect and what you need to offer in return. I've included three detailed case studies so you can see the different elements at play in navigating the application process and the pressures that the employer, recruiter and candidates face.

When you find a good recruiter and understand how they can help you, please share that knowledge with your friends and network. Your network and word of mouth are the best ways to find the right people to help you. I've included a guide to the templates for creating a spreadsheet of all the recruiters and network contacts you talk to and the outcomes, whether good or bad. This is the same one I have used for the past decade.

The principles of applying for a job remain the same. It does not matter whether you are looking for a contract role or a permanent role. You might apply for a job directly with an employer or use a recruitment consultancy. The lines might even be blurred with many large employers outsourcing their recruitment function to large recruiters.

So read the sections relevant to you right now. Drop in. Read a few chapters at a time. You do not need to read it cover to cover. You can also come back to it as you progress through your career.

The first two Parts of the book give you a behind-the-scenes guide to the recruitment industry and highlight the challenges that employers, recruiters and jobseekers face. Are you new to the world of job seeking? Maybe you've been in the same job for a long time? If so, these chapters will add perspective and explain the recruitment methods and systems in force today.

If you are well versed in the recruitment process but need guidance on making sure that you are in the top 1% of jobseekers you can go straight to Part 3, Managing Expectations.

I have also included short chapters for some of those less complex but frustrating topics such as how to negotiate and handle multiple offers or whether to disclose a medical issue.

A few years ago, a good friend of mine, Loren, twenty years younger than me and a successful entrepreneur, suggested there was no point in gaining all of this knowledge in life without sharing it. So here I am today writing this for you.

My career has taken me from being a young lawyer in London to interviewing UK cabinet ministers. I have built businesses in London, Sydney, Delhi and Bali across fashion, e-commerce, technology, recruitment. Today I specialise in career training and life transformation. Amongst that, I was a head hunter for 15 years placing jobseekers around the world. I have coached 'C' suite Executives from Fortune 100 companies to veterans going through career and life transition with complex trauma, and most people in between.

Some of you will have the fortunate position of multiple offers to decide between and I have included a few tips to help make that choice easier for you. But first there is one story I want to share with you. I had a client in London who was a large international law firm. They competed for recruits with their peers who had more money and more prestige. While their peers were complacent, my client would often roll out the red carpet in the recruitment process. Their peers would fly candidates out to London from Sydney for an hour long interview and then send them home. This firm would collect their interviewees from the airport and, for the 36 hours they were in London, they would immerse the candidate in their world, meeting partners, HR, and their future colleagues. My client took them out to hip restaurants for lunch and dinner and asked the candidates what they were excited about. They knew they could not match the salary and benefits, but they could offer a transparent place to work where people could thrive. Imagine how you, the jobseeker, would feel after such an immersive, honest, inclusive experience. As a recruiter, this client was a joy to work with. While not all recruiters you meet are blessed with deep client relationships, ask them as much as you can.

For you, the jobseeker, I would suggest getting behind the veneer of your potential employer. Get a feel for them, find out what makes them tick, what they are passionate about, where you fit into their future, and see whether that resonates with you. This is your career and the solution to finding what works for you is in asking good questions.

On a personal note I have battled and survived cancer and that journey taught me that there is plenty of hard work to do but that work is invaluable for succeeding in all aspects of your life. It is your birthright to create a life where you thrive so please make the best use of your time.

As the host of the Human Impact podcast I am lucky enough to share the stories of some of our most successful entrepreneurs, Nobel Nominated scientists, environmentalists, world champion athletes, Olympians, and humans dissecting some of the world's most significant challenges. What I learn from life is that when we find work that fulfils our mission and drives our passion and purpose, then doors open and opportunities abound.

PART 1:
THE RECRUITMENT INDUSTRY EXPLAINED

1.1 "THERE ARE FEW STANDARDS AND NO RULES"

When I started in the recruitment business over 20 years ago, the role of a head hunter was often steeped in mystery because we never talked about our clients or our candidates. In fact, some of my friends thought I was an arms dealer, such was the secrecy. We would, on pain of being fired, never reveal any details. This included the names of clients to candidates we considered a poor fit.

I share this with you because there are still a few old school, traditional, research-driven head hunters out there who charge up to 33% of your first year's salary, sometimes uncapped. These are the people to befriend. If you are lucky enough, they will be in touch. When that call comes, you know that your career has taken off and you are prized in the market. Nowadays, those relationships are easier to develop as technology has diluted the world of head hunting and executive search, and you are just as likely to be head hunted for a mid-level role as that of a CEO.

When I stopped practising law, I joined a high-end, boutique executive search practice in London where I spent four years learning the art and science of old school, research-driven head hunting. I ended up as a director, but my life had changed when my father died. I passed the last few months there staring out of the window with a gnawing feeling in my gut that I had to do something else and do it for myself. I empathise with those of you looking afresh at the possibilities for your life. Maybe you are ready to leave a job you have outgrown. Maybe it no longer serves you.

I wanted to have a look at the other side of the recruitment market before moving to Australia and setting up my own recruitment business, so I spent a short six months with a large volume recruiter based in London. There were 24 of us in a room around four huge desks. There was a bell on the wall which rang each time one of the team placed a candidate.

This new environment had far more energy but plenty of undiluted egos and a sense of 'just get the deal done'. The phone in the middle of each table chirped all day long. We would never answer it with our own names. Instead, we each had an alias. Mine was Rupert Black, a tongue-in-cheek reference to a character in Jilly Cooper novels. This may seem odd but it was common in recruitment; we had to make so many calls each day we would often call the same target company multiple times and they knew who we were. Sometimes the bankers we called treated it like a game and would say out loud: "There is a head hunter on the phone who wants to talk to me". We had to wear a thick skin and, as one of my earlier colleagues used to say: "Put your rhino hide on". Bankers took no prisoners.

In the world of head hunting, we only introduce a candidate with their agreement and can spend an hour and a half in an interview without disclosing the client's name. This volume recruiter expected me to forward candidates' resumes for roles, even if I had not asked them.

Management thought this was acceptable behaviour. They reasoned that if the jobseeker gave their consent once, then it was good for every occasion, even if it was six months earlier for another role. The policy was 'don't tell the candidate until we know they have an interview'.

I felt it was wrong and lacking in integrity, but that was my perspective and perhaps management thought I was sitting on my high horse. Integrity means something different to you compared to someone else. For me, it was the difference between creating deep relationships and short-term profit. Their thinking was simple; if we get the candidate into the role, we get paid and everybody is happy. We get to ring the bell which makes everyone work harder, even cut corners a little, in pursuit of money and bragging rights in the pub on Friday night.

Some of you may find nothing wrong with this while it may horrify others. The reason I share this is because, depending on your point of view, you should pursue the people who can help you with what you need today and what suits your own values and view of the world. There is no recruitment overlord judging your preference.

I know there are many sceptics about the recruitment industry. If you are one of them, I hope this book serves to show you that there are many professionals who want to help you with your career journey and will do an excellent job of that. It is about finding what works best for you.

There are few barriers of entry to this industry. Some recruiters and head hunters hold long careers in specialist fields before entering the world of recruitment. Others have none. Review recruiter profiles on LinkedIn and you'll see many with little life or work experience, or their earlier careers have nothing to do with the area of industry they now specialise in.

Some recruiters excel, but with no regulation, no experience, no money and no insurance necessary, anyone can set up a website on Wix, Weebly, Squarespace or Wordpress for free. In many cases they don't need clients or candidates on day one, yet they are now in business as a recruitment consultant.

That means you, the unsuspecting jobseeker, might apply for a job advertised by that recruiter.

The world changed forever after the Global Financial Crisis and Recession of 2007/2008, including employers trying to reduce recruitment costs. This resulted in the growth of internal talent acquisition teams and supplanted the use of external recruiters. To stay in the game, some recruitment business owners have lowered their prices to win work.

Heightened competition amongst recruiters to place candidates and meet their commission targets is one of the more obvious knock-on effects, coupled with pressure on management to increase profits. Many recruitment leaders believe the only solution is to drive down salaries. This results in lower quality recruiters who leave within a year or two anyway. When choosing, make sure you find a recruiter who can really help you.

The recruitment industry extends from retained head hunting, often with career professionals charging fees of 33% of the first year's salary, to contingent fees as low as 6%.

I have worked within a variety of recruitment models. Senior executive search, with exclusive retained assignments, could generate fees of 33%. A specialist volume recruitment business averaged fees of 20%. My head hunting companies in Sydney and Delhi charged between 20-25%. Some positions were exclusive, fewer retained, while the majority were paid on success.

There are inconsistencies in recruitment methods, revenue models and personal commission structures for recruiters. This contributes to the confusion around how the industry works, how recruiters can help you and what you can expect them to do for you.

In North America, it is common for recruiters to earn no salary at all. Instead they get paid on commission where they take home up to 50% of the fees they bring in. In Europe and Australasia, it is more common to earn a salary and commissions. I paid up to 50% commissions to my employees, even with a high base salary, though I know some recruiters who only receive a bonus based on the company performance.

As a jobseeker, you may well ask: "Why should I care?" As you will see from the case studies in Part 8, each of these recruiters have different drivers and motivations to help you. Some recruiters work on a handful of specialist assignments at a time and spend far more time with you, their candidate. Others may manage up to 20 campaigns at once with thousands of applicants, and they have little time to invest in you.

I was talking to the CEO of a well-known international recruitment business in London who was facing a slowing market and pressure from their new owners. They decided that the best way forward was to hire more junior recruiters, pay them less, reward them with lower commissions and increase their targets. You can only imagine how that story is unfolding. It is a fast drive to the bottom of a murky pond.

You may talk to one of those recruiters who face enormous internal expectations to place you and earn money for the company and themselves. It means customer service will fall short and ethical corners will be cut even though people still get hired through them and are happy to land that job. For everyone else, the experience is more likely to be negative.

1.2 THE $500BN RECRUITMENT INDUSTRY AND THE $1M A YEAR BILLERS

The recruitment industry can be lucrative and there are consultants who earn over $1m a year. Many more earn over $100,000 a year. The consultants in my head hunting business in Sydney used to earn between $400,000 and $500,000. They were in their late twenties, so this provided a fantastic lifestyle for them and their families. With no experience necessary to become a recruiter, it is not surprising that the industry attracts many people.

In the USA, the recruitment industry is worth $145bn each year. Globally, it is valued at over $500bn. The three biggest employment companies in the world, Manpower, Adecco and Randstad, contribute more than $70bn in total revenue and have over 100,000 employees between them.

In the UK, it is a £32bn industry with almost 40,000 registered recruitment businesses. In 2018, 8,000 new ones launched, though just as many closed within the first 12 months. Recent data in Australia shows there are 7,000 commercial recruitment businesses employing 93,000 people and generating $11bn in revenue.

You may ask why there is so much negative press about the recruitment industry. It is less to do with the hard-workers who put in long hours in pursuit of their fees and deliver a great service and more likely because of poor management and pressure to grow profit at all costs. However bad the reports are, these recruiters either have no time to do their job well or are under constant pressure to make the sale and that sale is you.

For all the candidates (which can be hundreds) applying for a job, only one will walk away happy. The recruiter has to manage the expectations of all the candidates including the unsuccessful ones.

My aim is for this book to guide you around the many pitfalls that can befall you on your job search and help you manage your expectations. Once you have that new role under your belt, you will soon forget any bad experiences. Maybe you will also pass on the details of those recruiters who have provided genuine support to you.

Remember: this is your future. It is more than just securing a new job today. The recruiter you didn't warm to could have the perfect opportunity for you in a few months.

Choose your recruiter carefully. If you were a parent, would you let someone care for your children with no references? Would you walk down a strange, dark alley on your own, late at night, in the rain, on your way back from a party? All your innate human warning bells would scream at you. You know that the likelihood of those situations working out well is low and the risk is not worth the short-term fix. Apply the same level of care and listen to those alarms when managing your career. Reflect on all contact with the recruiters and employer right up to signing the offer. If you have been in a toxic or unfulfilling environment before then ask yourself – am I asking the right questions now? What questions am I avoiding and why?

Act with integrity, even if those around you do not. Make it more of a mission and value for life rather than just part of your career journey today. In the next Part we take a deeper look at the current Recruitment Methods and Systems and provide a thorough understanding of what and who you will encounter on your job search process. If you are well versed in how recruiters work then skip ahead to Part 3, Managing Your Expectations or dive straight into Job Search Preparation in Part 4.

PART 2:
GUIDE TO RECRUITMENT METHODS AND SYSTEMS.

The recruitment industry uses many generic terms, which can often be confusing. Some of you may be familiar with the terms 'head hunter' and 'executive search' used in the business media when discussing hiring CEO's of Fortune 500, ASX 20 or FTSE 100 companies.

This section explains the recruitment processes associated with the different categories of recruiters and various systems, including technology, used by employers.

With this in mind you will find it easier to clarify the role your recruiter plays in the process and to understand how likely they are to secure an interview for you with their trusted client.

2.1 APPLICANT TRACKING SYSTEMS

When you submit your resume to an employer's website, you are likely to fill in an online form. This also applies to job platforms including LinkedIn when you use their native systems and the majority of public sector employers.

These systems are known as Applicant Tracking Systems. They filter your information according to the criteria set by the recruiter and the relevance of your application. You may be selected for an interview, allocated to a pending file, added to a talent pool, or your application may be automatically rejected.

I suggest that when you see a job advertised by an employer on a job board such as LinkedIn that you check to see if it is also advertised on the employer's website, and if so then submit your application on the employer's website. Their website will have more information about, and access to, the job, including clickable links highlighting selection criteria, more detail about the role, useful videos, and how to apply for the job.

You risk not seeing the complete job description if you apply from outside the employer's website. In addition, not following the correct process could mean your application is rejected at the outset.

2.2 CONSULTING

Consultants, for this guide, are not jobseekers but those individuals who offer their services as independent suppliers to as many clients as they like. I have consulted for many years to companies around the world from global enterprises to start-ups. As a consultant, you own your business and manage your own invoices and taxes.

Although consultants act independently they are sometimes prevented from working with their client's competitors. If you are a consultant, check the terms of your contract and take a practical and realistic view of how much work the client provides and the financial consequences of being not allowed to work for their competitors.

As a consultant, you are unlikely to interact with recruiters as you will find your own work. However, you still need to promote yourself and need to have a resume, bio, LinkedIn profile and be well prepared for interviews.

2.3 CONTRACT RECRUITMENT AND 'ON-DEMAND' WORK

A contractor is employed on a fixed term basis. That contract can be part-time or full-time and will always be for a fixed term. Sometimes this is extended or transferred to a permanent role, but you need to clarify this likelihood when you receive your offer. In most cases the contract is with the end employer; the company who you will work for.

With the rise of the freelance economy, there is a new breed of worker known as on-demand contractors. These people offer their services to one employer or several of them at the same time. Usually a labour hire company takes them onto the books and contracts them out to their clients for work when it is available.

Some of these labour hire companies offer zero-hour contracts where they guarantee no work at all but may also ask for exclusivity i.e. you cannot work for their competitors (though in my experience this is rare).

While contract recruiting is not new, there are some industries where 'on-demand' contracting is becoming commonplace, such as IT, technology, healthcare, construction, mining, law and accounting.

'On-demand' means that the recruitment businesses, or sometimes the end-employers who provide the services themselves, will have an ongoing requirement from their clients to supply staff on a project basis. You may be engaged for one day or a whole year.

As this work often requires people at short notice, some of these businesses will ask you to sign an exclusive agreement with them. For more detailed information on working with recruiters exclusively, see Part 9.

In most cases I have seen of on-demand contract work, the workers will invoice the employer (recruiter) and manage their own taxes.

2.4 EXECUTIVE SEARCH

Executive search is what it means; the proactive search to find executives for senior positions. Associated with firms such as Heidrich & Struggles, Korn Ferry, Russell Reynolds, and Egon Zehnder, these firms work on an exclusive and retained basis. They have research teams dedicated to mapping markets and finding the most suitable candidates. These firms do not advertise their roles and use head hunting as their method for identifying and screening candidates.

Search firms are also used for a variety of other reasons. It could be to replace an individual who has not yet been dismissed, to skill up and trade up in certain areas, to build a new team or further develop a division.

Businesses engage with search firms because they offer discretion, confidentiality, anonymity and can explore the market quietly and secretly. They can also gauge the reputation of a client or individual in a way that the business simply cannot do. They can also engage with candidates who might otherwise seem out of reach.

The assignment they work on is usually exclusive to them and no other recruiter can introduce a candidate to their client for that role.

The retained part means they are paid to carry out the 'search' in three stages:

- research
- shortlist
- offer

The fee is usually 30% to 33% of the first year's salary, though this is sometimes capped. In London in the 1990s, I worked on these types of roles where the total package often exceeded $5m.

If you are part of an executive search process, you will be one of a small number of candidates. At the shortlist stage you will be one of 4 to 6 candidates. Traditionally, the head hunters have no further interaction with their candidates after the process. This may seem harsh, but the candidates are linked to one assignment and executive search firms tend not to introduce candidates to other clients speculatively, though this is also changing.

The world of head hunting and how to manage working with head hunters is detailed in Part 6 and 7 and covered in the case studies in Part 8.

2.5 HEAD HUNTING

This phrase is used when any recruitment firm uses a proactive process of research to map the market and approach candidates. For example, they may contact you directly at work or through LinkedIn, rather than waiting for jobseekers to apply to a job ad.

2.6 LABOUR HIRE

This is a recruitment business which employs staff and then contracts them out on a labour hire agreement to their own clients. If you are offered a labour hire agreement, it means you will be employed by the recruiter, not by the company they send you to.

If directly employed by the recruiter, they will manage all of your pay and taxes, or you may be able to send them an invoice through your own company.

2.7 RECRUITER

This is the generic term for all recruitment consultants in every type of recruitment business, including executive search and head hunting, even though the executive search firms may not like it.

It is sometimes used to describe the internal talent teams of employers, but in this book it just relates to external third party recruiters.

2.8 RETAINED, CONTINGENT AND EXCLUSIVE

A retained recruitment assignment refers to a recruitment business being paid to find candidates for a specific role. It is usually exclusive. The recruiter tends to be paid upfront for the research and then on submission of a shortlist of candidates, regardless of whether the client hires any candidate. The final payment is made when the candidate starts their new job.

This type of recruitment is reserved for senior confidential positions or hard-to-fill roles where there is a lot of sensitivity regarding the hire.

An exclusive assignment means that only the contracted recruitment business may introduce candidates to their client. You will occasionally see on the bottom of a job advertisement a line such as "We are exclusively retained by X and all applications must be made through us. No other applications will be accepted".

If you are working with a recruiter who says they can make an application to an employer where there is already an exclusive mandate, then you need to tread carefully. In most cases, it is not possible. You should apply via the exclusive agency.

Contingent means the recruitment business is only paid on success. I often had assignments which were retained, exclusive to my company and which only paid on success.

2.9 RECRUITMENT PROCESS OUTSOURCING (RPO)

An RPO is a recruitment business normally contracted by enterprise-size employers to manage their external recruitment. The person managing your application is actually employed by a recruitment business, even though they work internally for the employer.

There are generally strict boundaries for these RPOs to avoid conflict. You could apply for multiple roles at one employer and have different recruiters from the same employer managing your application. Don't be put off by this. It is a normal, if puzzling, process.

2.10 TALENT ACQUISITION

Talent acquisition teams are the internal teams of employers responsible for external recruitment. If you apply for jobs directly, then someone in this team will manage your application.

If you are looking at making a direct approach to an employer, then develop a relationship with this team. Many of them are excellent and proactive at managing future hires.

2.11 VOLUME RECRUITMENT

This type of recruitment business manages large scale recruitment campaigns for multiple roles where there are likely to be many hundreds of applicants, typically for IT, healthcare, construction, admin and junior operational positions.

————

Now that you have a good understanding of how the industry works and the types of people, systems and processes you will come across in your job search, we can look at how to manage your expectations as this can be a frustrating process.

PART 3:
MANAGING YOUR EXPECTATIONS

3.1 THE WINNING FORMULA

As you embark on your job search, you may become frustrated by the recruitment and job search process. Our expectations of ourselves and others can be major contributors to frustration, anxiety, disappointment and unhappiness, not just in work and recruitment but in life.

Unless you land the very first job that you apply for, the recruitment process will disappoint you. Everyone has a different perception of the process based on their expectations and results.

The following formula can help you manage those expectations by assessing the probability of a likely outcome being met. *Four pillars govern the likelihood of that outcome:*

- Control
- Communication
- Knowledge
- Trust

If you imagine a dial between one and ten and apply it to each pillar, you can weigh up an outcome out of a total score of 40 by adjusting the dial for each pillar. If you score less than 20, your chances of that outcome being met are not favourable. Above 20, your chances are better.

Let me show you an example.

You are having a great interview. You make a personal connection with the interviewers. The role resonates well with you and they are trying to sell you the job rather than you selling yourself to them.

At the end of the interview, a member of the panel walks you back to reception saying "You will be fantastic for this role. You're just the type of person we want. I do hope you come and work with us. I'll be in touch with the recruiter later today and we can work out the details."

You walk away elated and wait for the recruiter to call. When they do, you are told that their client has hired someone else. You are crushed. You were not expecting that.

This example is extreme and as a human you will be disappointed. But let's apply the formula and see what happens.

Control: The only control you have in this process is to decide whether to accept their offer. They don't make one so the outcome is out of your control. The score is 0.

Communication: In this case they have communicated to you that they want to hire you, but there is no formal offer. The score is 8.

Knowledge: This depends on the quality of information the recruiter has provided about the process and the likelihood the employer will hire from this recruiter. It depends on whether they are looking at multiple candidates and considering internal candidates. If you are the second interview out of ten candidates, the dial is low. If you are the last candidate they see, it could be higher. I have coached jobseekers who were told they were the best candidate the interviewer had ever met and they would be a shoo-in for the job but they did not receive an offer. It happens. Let us say a score of 5.

Trust: Again, this depends on the relationship you and the recruiter have with the employer, in particular the interviewer. If the interviewer is the most senior person on the panel and has absolute sign off for the hire, your score could be high as high as 9, but if not, less than 5. Let us be generous and say 8.

The total score is 21 out of 40. The likelihood of that offer arriving is marginal and in no way a guarantee.

So while the interviewer's comment sounded great, discuss it with your recruiter to get a more balanced perspective.

You can apply this formula to everything in life from dating and business meetings to sales targets and securing a bonus or promotion. Manage your expectations in life. Make sure you communicate to others what you expect and why. Remember that this may have little bearing on whether they will be met.

3.2 WHAT RECRUITERS DO FOR YOU

There are several types of recruiter and each plays a different role in the recruitment process. As a general rule, manage your expectations by applying the following principles to finding the good ones.

Note, however, that a recruiter has to decide that your skills and experience are relevant to them first. Unless you a suitable candidate, you may hear silence in response to your job application or attempts to communicate with them.

What they will do:

- Open doors to employers
- Review your resume, online profile and LinkedIn information
- Manage your job application
- Give interview advice and interview guides
- Give salary advice
- Help negotiate an offer

What they will not do:

- Write your resume or LinkedIn profile
- Guarantee anything, from application to interview or offer
- Be your therapist

What they might do:

- Give career advice

Armed with this knowledge, the next section helps prepare for your first contact with recruiters or potential employers. For that you need to write a killer resume putting you in the top 1% of all jobseekers.

PART 4:
BEING IN THE TOP 1%;
WRITING A KILLER RESUME

4.1 THE MAIN ELEMENTS TO YOUR RESUME

On average, a recruiter will spend six seconds glancing at your resume. You need to make those six seconds count so they decide to read on rather than dismiss it.

If you submit your resume through an applicant tracking system (software used by job boards and many employers to screen and filter your application), be aware that a human may not view your resume until after the initial screening process. In some cases, where employers fully automate the process, the hirer may not review it until just before they walk into your interview.

That means you should write your resume so your skills and attributes address all the relevant selection criteria, including the exact keywords from the job ad, mirroring their words and phrases. The software programs are programmed to search for these keywords and rank applications based on how closely they match.

A professional resume writer can charge over $500 for a well-presented document relevant to your industry. If you hire one, know it is just the start as you will have to tailor each resume for each role you apply to. You will still have plenty of work to do.

There are some general rules to apply when writing your resume. While this book is not meant to provide a comprehensive resume writing service, the following tips will help you write one which gets attention and makes your application more interesting and more relevant.

Be specific. If someone else can write a similar sentence, paragraph or resume, then you are not being specific enough. Highlight what you have done and not your general skills. For example, *if you want to say you are an expert rather than write:*

"I have expertise in IT programming."

Instead write:

"I have 10 years' experience as a software engineer with X Company in Y role leading a team of 9 engineers in New York, Chicago while overseeing a team in Delhi, India."

One of the most important resume sections is about your key achievements. These need to be specific and measurable. Writing about your key achievements replaces a lengthy section on your current responsibilities. This is because there is little evidence to say you carry out the tasks your employer expects of you. Instead, listing your achievements substantiates your work as evidence you carried out your responsibilities.

As an employer, I expect you to have already faced and resolved some of the problems, tasks and challenges that I face in my business and that you can bring that knowledge to make an impact for me. That is your value and benefit. If you are not an experienced recruit, I want to know whether you have the ability, desire and motivation to learn, lead and share, and to become an asset to my business.

4.2 WRITING KEY ACHIEVEMENTS

Demonstrate your expertise in the key achievements section, which sits within your professional/work experience. What you write has a direct link to landing an interview and answering both technical and behavioural interview questions.

When you write strong key achievements, it serves two purposes for the recruiter and interviewer:

- They can instantly see what measurable results you have delivered and how these relate to the job they are looking to fill

- They can dive much deeper and faster into your expertise at interview. This allows more time to understand how you fit in rather than spending that time finding out whether you are technically qualified. It also frees up more time for you to ask questions.

For you, the jobseeker, this allows you to prepare better for interview questions. When you are familiar with your top four to five relevant achievements, these form the basis for most of your answers to behavioural questions, an area where people struggle the most at interview.

I suggest following the CAR method for writing key achievements and answering interview questions. CAR stands for Challenge Action Result and is similar to STAR which is Situation Task Action Result. Personally, I like to replace Result with Impact, but they both serve the same purpose.

A few tips for writing the best key achievements:

- The **Challenge** is the problem you faced and is the prelude to taking **Action** and solving the problem. The **Result** is the measurable impact and benefit from your action. Focus on the action and lead with descriptive verbs such as:
  - Led
  - Implemented
  - Managed
  - Increased
  - Organised
  - Sold
  - Reduced
  - Collaborated, etc.

- Focus on what you have achieved and not your team's achievements.

- Provide detailed examples, be specific and make them measurable if you can. Start sentences with action verbs, e.g.:
  - "Led and implemented a new accounting system which delivered a 20% increase in revenue collection within 30 days."
  - "Led the national sales team and grew sales revenue by $3m by implementing continuous training for all sales teams."

- Ideally you want 1-2 key achievements per year worked and a minimum of 5-6 per resume.

- Reflect on the proudest moments of your career:
  - When were your clients or managers especially grateful for your input?
  - Have you received company or industry awards?
  - What functional role do you perform every day?

- • Reflect on your tasks and activities and how you communicate with internal and external stakeholders.

- - If you have received an award, be specific about what project you were involved in that resulted in the award.

Remember this is your time to sell yourself, they cannot read what is in your mind, you have to tell them and be specific.

4.3 WHAT TO INCLUDE IN YOUR RESUME

Your resume should be a maximum of three to four pages long though a short one-page resume is fine for casual roles and where little experience is required. If you are looking for consulting work, you may create a "bio" which is a one-page condensed resume.

Include the following:

- Name, phone number, email and LinkedIn URL

- Career Summary: this summarises what you have done and can do. It is not a career objective. You can write this as paragraphs, paragraphs and bullets or just bullets, but my preference is paragraphs and bullet points. If you have a long career (15-20+ years) your first page could be taken up with your summary but make sure that your current professional experience is mentioned on the first page.

   The first line of your summary is the hook and should be the most impactful statement you write. Make it count and be specific. If the role requires certain skills then make sure you pre-qualify yourself as shown in the examples below.

- Professional Experience including dates (years are fine)

- Job title: make it similar and relevant to the role you are applying for as many employers have job titles which make no sense to the outside world.

- One sentence describing your current employer and what they do.

- One sentence detailing your current and previous roles and responsibilities: your Professional Experience comprises your achievements, i.e. what you have done rather than your responsibilities. Remember that employers want to see the value, benefit and impact you can bring based on your experience.

- Key Achievements: Refer to Chapter 4.2.

- Focus on the last 5 to 10 years and far less on older experience.

- Start your Professional Experience with your most recent experience first, and move chronologically through your experience.

- You don't need to list experience which is not relevant. For example, if you worked in retail ten years ago while at University, it is unlikely to be relevant now.

- Education, Certificates and Licences: showcase your education and qualifications after your professional experience. The only exception to this is where you need to pre-qualify your experience for the job. For example, if they require an MBA for the job, the first sentence of your Career Summary may read:

  "A Harvard MBA qualified..." This creates impact and grabs attention.

  It could be: "An award winning graphic designer..." or "An ITIL certified project manager with 8 years' experience..."

- You can also list your technical qualifications in your Career Summary after the first paragraph using bullet points, especially for IT and technology driven jobs.

- You don't need to list qualifications that are not directly relevant to your job.

- If you have Certifications which have expired, and are relevant to your job, you can list the date it was last current and add 'pending' or 'to be completed'. You can explain at the interview that you have had this certification and can renew it. Ask if they would prefer you did this before or after you start. Your new employer may even pay for it, and if not, you know what to do.

- Awards: if you have received an employer or industry award, then be specific about what it is and what you did to receive it. If you are the only person in the company to win one, then say so as it adds to your uniqueness. I have coached people who have won very prestigious awards such as veterans with Distinquished Service Medals and the Order of Australia but they did not promote these. If you have won an award which only a handful of people receive, it is an example of both your uniqueness and your outstanding unrivalled capability. Promote yourself. Differentiate yourself.

- Publications/Articles/Podcasts: if published in relevant publications or appeared on industry podcasts, then detail these.

- Voluntary Work: while all employers value the voluntary work you do, note that not every employer can honour your voluntary commitments. Large scale enterprise employers are more likely to have the back up in place to cover your absence due to voluntary commitments, whereas start-ups and small companies are not designed to cope with long or immediate periods of absence. In Australia, being a member of the Rural Fire Service is held in high esteem, but not all employers can accommodate extended periods of leave. Think about how important this to you and whether the job you are interested in can support you. If in doubt, ask.

4.4 WHAT TO EXCLUDE FROM YOUR RESUME

- Your address

- Your photo

- Acronyms: exclude acronyms because applicant tracking systems read letters as they are. Unless the employer or recruiter sets up a keyword search for the acronym, it will filter these out of the process and, despite having the skills, you may rank lower. I recommend including both the acronym and the full description (e.g. MBA– masters of business administration) so that the software programs have a choice of which keywords to select.

- Passions, interest, hobbies

- Referees details

4.5 REFEREES

You do not need to, and should not, list your referees on your resume.

Only disclose your referees when you get an offer. This way you don't breach the privacy of your referee before the recruiter needs to contact them. Otherwise, recruiters may add them to their database of potential clients or candidates before they need to. More importantly, this is about you controlling the recruitment process.

Recently, one of my clients missed out on a very senior role because their referee, who was disclosed too early in the recruitment process, was contacted 'quietly' before the interview. She rubbished the candidate and put herself forward for the job, which she was offered. This should never happen but it does, especially in industries and environments where the networks are strong. Employers will talk to their contacts, especially if those contacts have managed you, but you want to control this as best you can.

You need to select your referees with care for each job. Make sure they know you well, can vouch you are well qualified for the role, know your strengths and weaknesses and say that they would hire you again.

I once withdrew an offer from a jobseeker because their referee, who managed them in a start-up, suggested that in a start-up environment their expectations would be impossible to manage. Based on an earlier conversation with the candidate, I was alerted to this; the reference confirmed they would not be a good fit. Pick your referees wisely. If this candidate had given me another referee from another employer, I would have never known and might have employed him.

Find out when your referee will be available to talk to your potential employer and make it as simple as possible to contact them.

The only exception to providing your referee's details before the offer stage is when completing an online application form. Generally there will be a note suggesting they will not be contacted until the offer stage.

4.6 BEING THE OUTLIER OR 'LEFT-OF-CENTRE' CANDIDATE

Recruiters and employers alike often throw an outlier into the mix at the short list or interview stages. The outlier or 'left-of-centre' candidate is often immensely talented with a breadth of experience. They are often the mavericks, the entrepreneurs or those with a skill set an employer desperately wants and says they are interested in.

However, outliers are also the candidates employers rarely hire, sometimes because of fear of the unknown, sometimes due to internal politics and other times just because the employer wanted to have a look but never intended to make the offer.

Yes, they may be successful, but I estimate 90% of the time they are not. However, I know one recruiter who says that in the past six months 50% of all their candidates hired were outliers. However, it was for the Not For Profit industry which is experiencing huge commercial and regulatory changes; candidates from the private sector, with no NFP experience, were in demand.

There are always exceptions, but note that you do not want to be the outlier too many times. You will know when because either the recruiter will tell you or because you are called to an interview somewhat unexpectedly.

With a killer resume in your hand, there is just one more step before you can start applying for jobs. That key step is having a LinkedIn profile because that is where 99% of recruiters find you, the jobseeker. With both of these completed you are ready to contact recruiters, apply for jobs and control how you run your job search.

PART 5:

THE WHY AND HOW TO HAVING AN ONLINE PROFILE - LINKEDIN.

5.1 HOW LINKEDIN FITS INTO YOUR JOB SEARCH PROFILE

LinkedIn is not just a recruitment and job search platform. It is the most advanced social media and networking platform for professionals.

When I say professionals on LinkedIn, I mean that loosely. Some people in my network are not part of the corporate and professional services world. They are freelance designers, fashion designers, small business owners, artists, creatives, elite sportsmen and women, environmentalists and scientists. They all contribute because they are interested in conversing with their fellow humans. A job alone does not define your personality and soul.

I am an active user on LinkedIn and frequently post content related to my podcast, Human Impact, and my career training company, The Human Consultancy. But I estimate that 70% of all of my activity on LinkedIn goes offline; I take contacts made online to conversations offline and develop my network through email, Skype, Zoom and messaging.

The following helps put LinkedIn into perspective:

- There are 610m users with 20 million job vacancies in 2019.
  - 160m in North America
  - 60m in India
  - 28m in UK
  - 16m in Canada
  - 8m in Australia
- Having a link from your resume to your LinkedIn profile gives you a 70% better chance of getting an interview.
- Four times as many employers use LinkedIn to recruit from than any other social media platform.

- You are four times more likely to get a recruiter's call and nine times more likely to get hired when referred through a LinkedIn connection.
- Sending a personal and tailored written connection request is four times more likely to get accepted.
- Having a completed profile with the 'All Star' badge means you are 40 times more likely to get noticed by a recruiter. I explain 'All Star' badges later in this Chapter.

99% of recruiters use LinkedIn. It is now a must-have in your recruitment armoury and one day may replace the resume entirely.

That is just the start. Having the 'All Star' icon gives you an added edge. The badge appears on your profile under the 'About' section, usually at the right-hand side of your dashboard.

The 'All Star' tag in LinkedIn allows you to be more visible to external recruiters, internal talent teams of employers and can boost your profile when you apply for a job. LinkedIn will rank 'All Star' profiles higher than those without, meaning you get to the top of the queue.

LinkedIn is your opportunity to showcase your career and what you offer. You can promote yourself, in your voice, far better here than in a resume. You can add media, including images, PDFs and video, to both your summary and work experience to further showcase your work. If you have a website, add the link in your Summary and About sections.

It is up to you how you use your LinkedIn profile, though you should be aware that some employers have strict guidelines and legal restrictions about use of social media. If there are any restrictions that apply to you, please follow them.

You will see the progress bar on your profile move from beginner through intermediate to 'All Star' as you complete the sections below. When you have an All Star profile, a grey 'All Star' badge will appear.

One word of warning: like all social media platforms, LinkedIn adjusts their algorithms on a fairly frequent basis. What stands as we to go press may be different later, but if you cover all the bases below, your profile should still rank even if the algorithms change.

You can find my LinkedIn profile at https://www.linkedin.com/in/edandrew/

You can use it for some ideas if that helps and by all means connect and follow me as I share a lot of content there.

5.2 CREATING AN 'ALL STAR' PROFILE

1. Profile Photo: make it as professional as your job or industry expects.

2. Headline: this is searchable, so make your 120 characters count. Review commonly advertised job titles and use keywords related to jobs you want to get. Use job titles similar to those you are looking for so that your profile is matched closely to recruiters needs. Of course, only do this if you have the relevant experience to match the job title.

3. Summary/About: summarise your career highlights, what you are doing now, and where you want to go. Tip: you have only 3 lines visible on a desktop PC before 'read more' and on mobile devices only 20-30 words so make them stand out. Your first sentence should be a hook. Make it specific and unique to you. Never be generic. You have a maximum of 2,000 characters.

4. Employment/Professional Experience: make sure that when you search for your employer, past or present, you tag their name to your profile. (The icon for their company will be displayed). This makes your experience with your employer searchable, whether it is current or previous. Recruiters will search for people who have worked for specific companies. If you are no longer working, LinkedIn does not allow an 'All Star' profile (at the time of this book going to print). I recommend you create a new employer for yourself as a freelancer. For example, I would be Ed Andrew Consulting. This way LinkedIn will allow you to keep your ranking and you may also attract freelance work while you are looking for a job. It is fine to say: "Currently freelancing while looking for my next permanent or contract role"; recruiters will know you are still open to opportunities.

Make sure you complete the Job Title field and remember this is still keyword searchable, so make use of the space. Also add some experience. You can take this from your resume and you can break down your experience as you progress through your employer to reflect time spent in different roles and promotions.

5. Skills: you need five but can add up to 50 skills.

6. Certificates and Licences: add these to make you more relevant and searchable (though at the moment you don't need them for an 'All Star' profile).

7. Education: you need this so add a course you have completed, such as University or Higher Education, even High School is needs be and tag the Education provider because it is searchable by recruiters.

8. Recommendations: this is a field which used to be required for an 'All Star' profile. I suggest you complete it as LinkedIn may reinstate this. In the 'Skills' section, other people can add you as an expert with no input from you but in the 'Recommendations' section you will need to send a request and also accept them when given. The process is managed entirely through LinkedIn and requires action by you. My suggestion is to get three or four work colleagues you are close to and provide them to each other. These are not formal work references; they are more like testimonials. You could get them from fellow employees, suppliers, customers and people who attended your seminars, workshops or, in my case, podcast guests.

5.3 CONTACTING RECRUITERS AND EMPLOYERS

Once you have set your profile up, you can start sending connection requests to your colleagues and those you want to network with.

A few tips:

- Always send connection requests with a personalised message rather than the generic default.

- Be clear about why you want to connect, especially with potential future employers.

- 'Inmail' is different from 'Messaging'. You can send as many messages as you like to 1st degree connections, but 'Inmail' is limited by the type of account you have.

- Recruiters are more likely to accept your connection request than reply to messages. This is simply due to the volume of messages they receive. The good ones will monitor their messages daily.

- Check a connection's activity (posts, likes and comments) before you send a message. You can view their activity on their profile page. If a user has an inactive profile and has turned off their notifications, they may never know you sent them a message until they log in to their account. Manage your expectations wisely.

5.4 MANAGING LINKEDIN MESSAGES FROM RECRUITERS

If you want recruiters to find you, having a relevant and complete 'All Star' profile on LinkedIn and showing your profile as 'open to recruiters' means you will receive messages and requests from them.

Having skills which are in high demand by employers further increases your likelihood of being contacted by recruiters.

My suggestions for dealing with these messages are common sense. You will receive generic messages if you come up in a filtered search for keywords your profile matches. The recruiter may take one step further and send a personalised connection request to you.

Your time is as valuable as theirs, so decide who you want to connect with. If the recruiter is well known in your sector, this may be the perfect time to speak to them. Remember that you are looking to build relationships with two to three really good recruiters who can help throughout your career.

- Do not assume that because they sent you a polite message and seem to know what you do, that they will be a relevant recruiter for you. Ask the right questions and make an informed decision.
- If it is a generic or personalised message and not in your area of expertise, delete it or ignore it.
- If you receive a generic message where it identifies roles that you are looking for, have a look at their profile and company and make an informed decision if you think they can help you. If you do talk to them, ask the right questions. Never send your resume before having that conversation.

- When you receive a personalised message which identifies jobs that you are looking for, or even if you are not really looking but the jobs are in your area, then I suggest reaching out if you think they can help you now or in the future.

Note that you do not need to feel pressured to reply or reach out. These messages are unsolicited. You did not ask for them. If you have no interest, you can just ignore them.

5.5 USING LINKEDIN WHEN YOU HAVE A 'SIDE GIG'

I am often asked what a LinkedIn profile should best promote and showcase, especially for those who are building a side gig while continuing to work part-time or full-time. It is for you to decide what purpose your profile serves and what benefit you want from it. You may just want to use it to get a job, so create your profile for that purpose, especially if you cannot find work easily through your network. When you have found a job, you can change it and use it to promote your business.

Consider your financial needs first and if you need LinkedIn to find a job, I suggest you write a profile first and foremost which covers the bases and gets you noticed for a job. If you confuse recruiters or employers by looking like an entrepreneur, they will likely skip on by.

As an employer and ex head hunter, I can assure that uncertainty breeds distrust. Both recruiters and employers will stay well away from people looking for permanent jobs who, by glancing at their resume or profile, look like they want to run their own business. The belief is that you will leave soon and not dedicate enough time to them.

If you want a side gig, or are building a business, make this clear on your profile if it does not compromise your chances of getting employed work.

A final point is that recruiters may also try to get you to draft a profile that serves them and their clients. This is not always possible simply because you may be working with several who all want something slightly different. In this case, make it very clear on your profile what you are looking for and cover as much ground with your skills and experience as you can. LinkedIn is your chance to promote yourself however you see fit.

5.6 FINAL TIPS

Note that my LinkedIn URL is unique to me:

https://www.linkedin.com/in/edandrew/

If you do not have your own website or a strong personal brand, then most likely this will be the first appearance of your name in Google search, so make it count.

The LinkedIn URL allocated to you might look like this:

linkedin.com/in/jane-smith-kcfegt177785

… and it is not so easy to find.

You can edit your URL in "edit public settings" under privacy settings. Try to get your name to match you as closely as you can. If you have a common name like Jane Smith, then you could use a middle name or initial, or tailor it to your profession, e.g. if you are an engineer, you could be /janesmithengineer/

You can also follow LinkedIn's own guide to editing your URL as they change the settings from time to time:

https://www.linkedin.com/help/linkedin/answer/87/customizing-your-public-profile-url?lang=en

One of the important privacy settings that you want to be aware of is your ability to let recruiters know that you are looking for a job. LinkedIn has changed the 'Career Interests' section to be on your 'My Profile' page and you will find the settings there. Only you can see this. While recruiters will know that you are open to opportunities, it is not a public setting. While you are job searching, make sure you switch on the setting 'Looking for job opportunities'. Note that sometimes LinkedIn changes the wording of this setting.

With your killer resume and LinkedIn profile set up, and for those of you who are active jobseekers and have enabled those privacy settings, you can start to find recruiters and apply for jobs.

PART 6:

FINDING RECRUITERS AND APPLYING FOR JOBS

6.1 WHAT EMPLOYERS LOOK FOR

Employers, and by default their recruiters, are looking for three key elements from jobseekers:

- Can you demonstrate why you love them and want to work for them?
- What value and benefits do you bring?
- What positive impact will you make?

Culture and fit play a major part too, including how long the future employer thinks you will stay with them and whether they can meet your career aspirations. ***We can also add a fourth key factor:***

- Are you aligned to their values and mission?

To secure an interview, you and your resume will be judged on the first three. The fourth will be considered at interview and in conversations with the appointed recruiters. This last element is also what you should reflect on when deciding whether to accept a job with them. You need to ask good questions at interview to see how they will support you and whether their style of work and values suit yours.

As an employer, I break these elements down into two attributes.

- Are you relevant and suitable?

The first three key elements are best summarised by your relevance. Your skills, strengths, experience, leadership ability, emotional intelligence and ability to learn, contribute to your relevance to a future employer. In short, do you have the hard and soft skills they are looking for?

To me, suitability is defined by your desire, motivation and character. Are you somebody they want in their team for the time they have determined is commercially viable? How long will you stay? Are you a future leader? If you rock the boat, will it be worth the pain? More than all of that, what I want is energy, passion and enthusiasm.

As an employer myself, these are the questions I ask and the attributes that I look for. You will need to prove that you are both relevant and suitable to land a job.

Now you know what employers are looking for, you need to get in front of them. You can do that either through a recruiter, though your network or making a direct approach.

6.2 GETTING ACCESS TO RECRUITERS

If you want a recruiter to arrange an interview for you, there are four paths to working with them:

- Getting head hunted
- Applying for a job managed by a recruiter
- Approaching a recruiter
- Asking for a referral from a friend

The word 'head hunted' has been diluted over the past fifteen years and as discussed in Parts 1 and 2, it means one of two things:

1) You are at a stage of your career where the global head hunters and independent executive search boutiques have you on their radar for specific jobs and you will be one of a select group of people approached for one job at a time.

2) On LinkedIn, your profile has come up in the search filters and recruiters reach out to see if you want to talk. (LinkedIn is covered comprehensively in Part 5. If you work in the corporate world or your customers hang out there, it is the place where you want to have an up-to-date profile and an active presence.)

Ideally, you want to develop relationships with at least three to four recruiters or head hunters who you get to know well and will support you throughout your career.

The three detailed case studies in Part 8 reflect candidates who have followed all four paths; they have been head hunted, approached the recruiter, applied directly for the job or been referred by friends.

In the case study of Cassie Stone, friends referred the candidates to the recruiter. Aside from being head hunted directly, this is the primary method you want to use if you can. The benefit to you is that a referral creates more immediate trust, comes with knowledge of how the recruiter works and gives you the inside track on how they can best support you. It also means that you can make fewer applications with a greater chance of success.

The benefit to the recruiter is that you, the jobseeker, are less likely to be shopping around so they have a greater chance you will accept an offer through them and they will get their fee.

6.3 BECOMING VISIBLE

You know you need recruiters to discover you but if you have not yet had any calls it could be for a number of good reasons:

- Your profile on LinkedIn could be incomplete or fairly new and has not yet generated any hits from recruiters
- You could work in a very specialist area that recruiters don't work in...
- ...or a very generalist area where there is no shortage of candidates
- You could be positioning yourself for a different career path
- You could be a mum or dad returning to work after raising children
- You could be a graduate
- As in the case of many people I have coached, you could be a military veteran seeking a new career having served your country

If you fall into one of these categories, then the next few chapters will help you find a recruiter. I understand that the job search process can be daunting and for some, especially after a redundancy, it can be overwhelming. I intend to make it simple and painless so you can move forwards in your job search with confidence.

6.4 NETWORKING AND ASKING FOR HELP

In the third Case Study in Part 8, about Tammie, I share the example of when I was in London after many years away and needed to build my network to find consulting work. I had to approach an old school friend who I had not spoken to in over 30 years. It filled me both with dread and excitement, but it led to two lucrative pieces of work.

While this part of the book is about how to find recruiters, I want to stress again that the best way is through people you know. Often that means asking for help from your network, however uncomfortable that may be. If someone asked you for help, what would you say? I am sure the answer is yes.

If you are not working and you have a social media account, especially Facebook or LinkedIn, ask your network for suggestions. Remember, your friends want to help. If you have drawn a blank, then start finding recruiters yourself.

If you want to take a deeper dive into the world of networking, then I recommend listening to episode 99 of my podcast Human Impact where I talk to networking guru David Burkus, author of *"Friend of a Friend"*.

6.5 PREPARATION AND RESEARCH

Start your preparation by creating a spreadsheet where you list the recruiters and the jobs you apply for. I suggest you include:

- Name of recruitment firm
- Name of person
- Phone number
- Email
- Date contacted
- Method of contact i.e. phone or email
- A brief note of any correspondence
- Any referrals they gave to you to other recruiters
- The date you submitted your resume
- The job you submitted your resume for
- Progress of your application

For applications you make direct to employers, record:

- Name of employer
- Name and details of contact
- Date of communications
- Brief note of conversations or emails
- Date of application
- Any time/dates they suggested for the process
- Interviews and names of interviewers
- Feedback from interview—yours and theirs

I still have a spreadsheet I created over ten years ago when moving between London and Sydney. On this document, I also included any networking contacts I made and referrals I was given. I suggest you do the same as you never know when you might use it again.

Remember that this is the part of the process where you are actively looking for work. Before you start, you will need your resume and most probably a LinkedIn profile in place. Any recruiter you talk to will want to see your work experience and if you have not created these already, they will ask you to provide them soon.

The exceptions to this are:

- When you have been head hunted and may not need an active resume
- Where you want to start a conversation with a recruiter to get some guidance on your skills and job search

Be careful as a recruiter's time is precious and limited; not all will want to invest in you unless you have specific skills their clients' are seeking and they can see the benefit of working with you.

To find recruiters, go to places where they advertise their jobs or their services and have an approach relevant to your individual job search. *The methods I recommend are:*

- Google: Run a Google search based on your specific industry and jobs that you are looking for, such as 'corporate lawyer jobs in Sydney', 'contract accounting jobs in New York', or 'business development manager jobs in London'. Be as specific as possible, even if you run more general searches later. I am sure you are all familiar with Google search and the two types of results; the paid 'ad' results where recruiters are advertising to get your attention and the 'organic' results where companies have worked hard to achieve the top spot to grab your attention. Do some research on all of them and if they have jobs that may be relevant to you, add them to your list.

- LinkedIn: If you are looking at corporate and professional jobs then I suggest that LinkedIn (with over 20m vacancies globally) is a great place to start. You will need a LinkedIn profile to access these. See Part 5 on how to set up a LinkedIn profile and how to manage recruiters on LinkedIn. While you cannot yet filter via salary bands, it has good refined job search tools. You can see how long the job has been posted for, how many people have applied, and sometimes the person who posted it. If you have a LinkedIn Premium profile, you can see how strong your application is compared to others.

- Job Boards: While some job boards and aggregators such as Monster and Indeed are global, others are more regional such as Seek in Australia, Careerbuilder in US, Reed or totaljobs in the UK, and Naukri in India. You can also find industry specific job boards and I suggest running Google searches for these to see if they are relevant to you. When you find jobs you would either like to do or are matches for your skills and expertise, make a note of the recruiters advertising the roles. Put them on your list and do your research. Look at their websites and LinkedIn profiles, then contact them. You can also look at sites such as Glassdoor which review employers and have their own job boards.

- Look at the large global recruiters like Manpower, Randstad and Adecco to see if they are relevant to your job search.

6.6 CONTACTING THE RECRUITERS

Once you have identified several recruiters advertising the kind of jobs you are interested in, you can assess:

-   Which ones to approach
-   How helpful they might be
-   Which jobs you may apply to anyway

You can contact recruiters in several ways:

-   Phone
-   Email
-   LinkedIn messaging and sending connection requests
-   Applying for a job

Your experience and interaction with recruiters will depend on your perspective, your expectations and the type and nature of the jobs you are applying for. The case studies in Section 8 have many 'pro tips' to help you navigate this process. They also include questions to ask the recruiters to determine how professional they are.

For instance, if you are looking at a short-term contract role to cover some time before deciding on your next career move, you may find that the process is quick and you have little interaction with the recruiter. If they are professional and deliver what they said, that is a good experience, even if all they say is "I will only get back to you if you get an interview and that will be within ten days".

Being a jobseeker is about asking good questions and having the best information available to make decisions.

If you have reasonable expectations, the process is less likely to frustrate you.

On the other hand, you may well have been head hunted for a senior role where the process takes six months to complete and you have hours of conversations with the recruiter. If you get the job and accept it, then your perception may differ from those who did not.

If you are being head hunted, the recruiter will likely advise you how long the process may take so you are prepared for it. *The recruiter's job is a fine balance of:*

- Keeping their client informed
- Managing their client's expectations around hiring the right candidate
- Managing the internal politics surrounding the job search and the respective candidates
- Managing the expectations of you, the jobseeker

Most head hunters are highly experienced with a powerful knowledge of your industry and are absolute professionals. One thing I can pretty much guarantee is that they are masters of discretion and confidentiality.

In the next part (which includes a chapter on registering your resume), we explore the ways to submit your resume for a job, or register for a general talent pool with a recruiter or job board. We look at what can happen to your resume after you have submitted it, the questions to ask to determine whether the recruiter can help you and what they will do with your resume and personal information. It is your resume and your future. Make sure you make wise choices based on good information.

6.7 INCREASING SUCCESS - WHICH JOBS TO APPLY FOR?

One of the hardest tasks when you are looking for a job is to restrain yourself from applying for too many jobs in the hope that success is a numbers game. It is not. All you do is to waste time and energy and become frustrated by the process. I am well aware that if you send off 50 applications and get one good job offer, then you can forget about the 49 rejected applications. However, that is also 49 applications to future potential employers who have now rejected your application.

The golden rule is that if you meet 70% of the selection criteria for a job, then you can apply. 70% is pretty much standard across the recruitment industry because it is almost impossible to find a candidate who ticks every single box. There is always some flexibility.

The fewer attributes you have that match the keywords and experience the employer is looking for, the lower the chance you have of being interviewed or your application being accepted.

If the 30% that you do not match are the 'must haves' such as certain technical skills, specific management or operational experience, qualifications or certifications then it is more likely the hirer will reject your application.

Regardless of whether the process is being managed by a recruiter or a named internal talent acquisition consultant, if in doubt, contact them and ask.

I suggest you list the key selections criteria from the job ad, including:

- The 'must haves'
- The 'nice to haves'
- Qualifications
- Operational and management experience
- Technical skills
- Soft skills such as emotional intelligence, communication, negotiation, stakeholder management

Against that list write down your skills relating to each, including supporting examples (e.g. key achievements that are discussed in more detail in Part 4). See what percentage of the requirements in the job description you meet. Anything above 70% means that if you apply, you have a reasonable chance of landing an interview.

For Entrepreneurs

As entrepreneurs, we believe we can apply ourselves to anything, especially when we need some work before embarking on our next project. However, I have learned somewhat painfully over the years, while we may have this attitude, few traditional employers think the same way.

You are not unemployable, but you need to be structured and careful with how you write your resume and what skills, achievements and strengths you highlight. The most obvious and frequent comment is "How long before you start your next business?" or the unsaid comments which are "How long before you want my job?"

If you have had a long career and covered many roles, both specialist and generalist, the tendency is to apply for everything; you have done 40-50% of it before and you believe that you can skill up on the rest easily.

Writing a resume this way and applying for many jobs you think you can do just leads to frustration because the less selection criteria you meet, the less likely you will be asked to an interview.

If you are an entrepreneur looking to return to employment or you are looking to change your career path, there are jobs out there, but you need to tailor your specific skills when making those applications. Carefully frame your resume and LinkedIn profile to show you want to work full-time again.

Obviously, if you are looking for short-term work or contract work, the two points above are less relevant, but your skills still need to match what employers and recruiters are looking for. My final recommendation is that your network will often be a far richer source of work and information than the open market. As I have mentioned before, do not be afraid to ask for help from your network.

We have explored the three main factors that employers are looking for in their next recruits and you can use these to determine whether you have the relevant skills that they are looking for.

If you have established a relationship with a good recruiter and they have advertised a role you like, this is the time to ask them whether your skills are relevant. As they know you, you can also ask how suitable you are for the role. If you have a trusted relationship with them, then you can expect guidance and also their view on your probability of landing an interview and getting hired. *When I was head hunting, we always had four prerequisites for each job:*

- Employer
- Specialist area
- Length of service in that area
- Qualifications

If a candidate could meet all four, we knew they had a 70% chance of landing an interview and that such a candidate could get hired based on their skills and suitability.

You may ask why there was only a 70% chance. It comes down to twin factors of the hiring process:

- Whether the job spec is changing at the client's end
- The human nature of the people involved, which usually means seeing something in your resume they like or dislike that is entirely subjective.

As a head hunter I could influence those initial decisions based on long term trust and having built a very strong client relationship, a partnership. You want to work with similar recruiters.

6.8 WHY COVER LETTERS ARE IMPORTANT

I coach many people, both senior executives and younger professionals, and, before I work with them, they have often already applied unsuccessfully for many jobs.

The most frequent reasons their applications are rejected are:
- They do not have the relevant skills needed for the job
- They do have the skills but their resume and cover letter have not addressed the selection criteria properly and are too generic

The real opportunity to put yourself and your personality forwards is with your cover letter. *Here you can address the selection criteria from your own point of view, including:*
- Why you want to work for them
- How your skills match their needs, showcasing examples
- How you will make a difference

As an employer, I always expect a cover letter. If you write a great one which grabs my attention, then I am likely to interview you. If you don't write one, then unless you have something exceptional in your resume, your application will be in the 'no' pile. If you write one which has obviously been sent to many others and doesn't address my company specifically, then it will also be in the 'no' pile.

If you are applying for a job advertised by a recruiter, you usually don't need to send a cover letter. This is because your application goes to the recruiter and not the employer, their client. However, always check. If the recruiter requires one, write a cover letter customised to the selection criteria within the ad.

The next phase of your job search is to put your toe in the water and start to make applications. It is this stage which can cause the most frustration, anxiety and uncertainty. Some of you will only want to apply reactively and others will want to maintain a proactive, ongoing job search. Managing these processes requires both skill and knowledge to overcome the many hurdles and unfamiliar ground that you will cover. Part 7 will help you navigate this.

PART 7:
EXPANDING YOUR JOB SEARCH, USING JOB BOARDS AND TALENT BANKS

7.1 REGISTERING YOUR RESUME

Now that you have written an excellent resume and decided which recruiters to work with, or which employers to apply to directly, you can start the application process.

When you are looking for a job, there will probably be several recruiters working in your niche area, all advertising jobs which interest you. It is also likely they will ask you to register or submit your resume and profile with them. You may want to do this to keep up-to-date with new job openings or to register your interest and apply for a particular job.

This can be a normal part of the registration process for each recruitment company, but it can be hard to navigate because there are no universal standards in place. You will need to check each recruiter to determine how they will treat you professionally, legally and ethically.

If you fall into the trap of registering your resume with recruiters without knowing how they use your information, they could send out your resume to your dream employer without you ever knowing about it. This employer might reject your application because it has not been tailored to be relevant to them, thus wrecking your chances of landing that dream job.

Registering your details is a normal part of the recruitment process and something that you should explore. It is tempting to register your resume with a number of recruitment companies in the hope they notice your skills and call you back about a position that they have. It may happen, but you need to know how they can help you.

Registering your details usually means two separate processes:

1) Sending (registering) your resume and details to a recruitment agency. You can do this via email or by filling out an online form on their website. For a general registration of interest, you have probably not applied for any jobs. However, if you register your resume regarding a specific job, then you will almost certainly have 'applied' for that job through the recruiter's website. This does not mean the employer, if they are genuine, will ever see your resume. All you've done is put your resume into the hands of the recruiter who will determine your suitability and manage your application. It is still a lottery over which you have virtually no control. This is where perspective plays a part. If you are a candidate whose experience is a good match regarding relevance and suitability, then you will get a call back from the recruiter. If not, you may never hear from them again. As a jobseeker you will either be happy and engaged, or ghosted.

2) A recruiter registers (submits) your resume with a client for a role. You have applied for a job through them.

   Both stages are normal when done with the correct intent and professionalism. Recruiters rely on their database of talent to identify candidates with speed and ease so they can match and present to their clients. Registering your resume adds to this talent pool.

   Some recruitment companies take a proactive approach and search the market rather than relying on inbound job applications. They typically have no mechanism or desire for candidates to register their resume. They prefer to head hunt them and filter those who apply to job ads before entering them into a database. On the other hand, I once advised a recruitment business who used no filtering; their database was clogged up with candidates who had no relevance to their clients.

While I have not registered my resume with any recruiter since I was 20 years old, I have certainly sent my resume to a recruiter to assess my suitability for a job. Even when I have said "This is not an application but just for your reference", I have still received an email back saying: "Thank you for submitting your resume to 'X'. We will be in touch once our client has selected a shortlist".

Now you can put that down to a recruiter being so busy that they don't read their emails or conclude that this is how they treat your data. Either way, they believe once you send your resume it is no longer yours but theirs to do with as they wish. In my view, this is never acceptable, so please do not let them pressure you into thinking it is OK just because the recruiter takes a position of power over you.

Recruiters have insights, knowledge and the key to the door, but they do not own your data. It is your resume and your career.

7.2 THE SHOTGUN APPROACH: LOSING CONTROL

By now, you may have registered your resume or applied for an advertised job with a recruiter but don't yet know the employer's name. The shotgun approach is where this recruiter sends out your resume to as wide an audience as possible in the vain hope that they may get a hit.

This registration of your resume with their clients has one objective in mind; to have your details on their client's database before anyone else registers you. They do this not to assist you with your job search but to prevent any other recruiter from representing you. Normally, if your resume has been entered into an ATS (applicant tracking system) or received by a client, it means that if you accept a job with that client within the next six to twelve months, they will be paid and not anyone else. You may well ask: "What is wrong with this if it finds me a job?"

Imagine this scenario: Toby from TC Consultants (see the case study of Cassie Stone Part 8) sends your resume to Alltech. There is no current job and the recruiter may be a preferred supplier or have no real relationship with them. There is no interview, feedback or interest. Effectively your application has been rejected because there was no job. I should add that savvy employers know this and can reject the application based on the fact it has no merit, but remember it has your name attached to it.

Four months later the perfect job comes up with Alltech and a head hunter has approached you with whom you have been talking for a long time and built up trust. They cannot represent you unless you go back to Toby and ask him to withdraw your application from Alltech. If you ask him, then he must do it, but he will put a huge amount of pressure on you not to do so. This is unethical and unprofessional. It is your career, your choice and you have the freedom to ask and do as you wish. Do not let anyone take that away from you.

Again I hear some people saying: "Well, they may still get me the job". Yes, that is true but they have also established that they have a weak relationship with their client, that they do not have your back, have not even told you about this new role and probably cannot negotiate well on your behalf. They are only interested in your ability to make them money.

If you want to have your resume sent to every company, that is your right. Maybe you must leave your current position now, or you are looking for a role overseas. However, in my experience, it is unlikely that many of those employers will interview you or offer you a job. They are all looking for slightly different skills, experience, ability and cultural fit which boils down to how well your application is tailored to show your relevance and suitability to them.

I have seen many excellent candidates sucked into 'the resume registration game'. I suggest that, first, you establish your priorities, your goals and what you want to achieve, then apply to a few at a time. Be aware that a recruiter may well try to pressure you into applying for many roles at once, as they will be afraid that you may either apply by yourself or apply through another recruitment business. The good ones will develop a relationship with you and tell you honestly what they can and cannot do to help you.

There is nothing wrong with a recruiter representing you and making a speculative application to a client who the recruiter knows well, or even making one when they don't them well. What ethical recruiters do is give an overview of your experience without compromising where you work or your name. That way if their client, the employer, cannot progress your application, the client never knows who you are and you can apply afresh to that company in the future.

7.3 TALENT BANKS: CREATING A PROFILE ON AN EMPLOYER'S CAREER SITE

There are three talent bank categories that you can consider registering your resume with:

- An employer's career site and talent pool
- A job board
- A recruiter's database

We have covered registering your resume with a recruiter. You may find it useful to be on a recruiter's database so they can notify you when a new suitable job arises. It is entirely up to you how you manage this and how much control you have over your resume. Just because your resume is on their database does not mean that they will send it out without your consent. Neither does it mean you will hear from them again. Your decision will be influenced by whether this is a short-term job search or part of managing a long career.

A talent bank is a pool of jobseekers' resumes that either recruiters or employers can access. When you apply directly to an employer's website, they may ask you in the application process whether you want to add your resume and profile to their pool of candidates. If your application is unsuccessful for one particular role, or when there are no suitable roles, your resume and profile are available in case another opportunity arises where they may consider you.

If you are applying directly to an employer and consider them aligned to your values and job search mission, there is no harm in having your profile registered with them. You can always login and remove it later.

7.4 APPLYING ON JOB BOARDS AND REGISTERING YOUR PROFILE

If you apply for a job on a job board, there are three outcomes:

- Your application is managed through the job board
- Your application is re-directed through to the employer's website
- Your application is re-directed to the recruiter's website.

Applying for a job and registering your profile and resume on a job board are usually two separate processes. You don't need to create an active profile before applying for jobs on many job boards, but most will require completion of some type of online application form.

Registering your profile and resume on a job board can be a productive process but, as always, you need to understand how they will treat your data. In my experience, job boards are far more transparent about managing your information than recruiters. While job boards are not regulated, millions of eyes are watching them, meaning they are more careful and compliant with privacy laws.

The technology company I built a few years ago was a peer-to-peer recruitment marketplace with a talent bank and job portal where you, the jobseeker, had complete control over the process. Most of the leading job boards have adopted that methodology today.

Benefits of registering a profile with a job board or talent bank include:

- You control your resume and profile
- You may be able to control whether recruiters or employers can view your details together or separately

- You may be able to see who has viewed your details and how often
- With automation and job matching, your job search continues while you sleep
- You can communicate directly with employers and recruiters though the platform

- You can receive email job alerts

Negatives include:

- Your own employer may be able to see you have registered and in the talent pool looking for a job
- Unscrupulous recruiters may use your information without your consent
- You may end up on many recruiter's databases without knowing it

7.5 PRO TIPS FOR USING JOB BOARDS

Before registering your profile, find out what that means. Are you included in the talent pool? Who can view your profile? Do you get access to email job alerts? How is your data used? What are the benefits?

You can sometimes:

- Create email alerts without registering a full profile.
- Apply for jobs without registering a full profile.

You should:

- Carefully check which resume and cover letter you upload for each application because some job boards will create a default resume or will upload the previous one used. This means your resume and cover letter which you customised for Employer X could go to Employer Y. This will almost certainly end in a rejected application.
- Tailor your resume to suit the job selection criteria for each application, including your customised cover letter.

If a job is advertised on a job board and an employer's own career site, make the application on the employer's career site only. There are three reasons for this:

- The number of words is often limited on a job board advertisement so you may not see the full job description
- Many job boards do not allow clickable links which may include advice on how to apply, the formats (Word or PDF), whether you need to write a cover letter, key selection criteria and a more detailed description

- Often you can see contacts for the talent acquisition or HR team and videos of the team you are applying to join. In short, there is often far more information available to you on employer's career sites.

I recommend you always submit your resume in Word, not PDF, unless the job ad specifically asks you to do so. This is because the software used by applicant tracking systems within job boards and employers career sites is better programmed to read keywords in Word documents than PDFs. You stand a better chance of your resume being correctly filtered and landing that interview.

7.6 WORKING WITH RECRUITERS: ASKING GOOD QUESTIONS

Ask good questions to discover who can help you and whether you want to trust the recruiter with your job search. ***Be flexible and apply this formula:***

- Research – gather information, look at their website, social media, LinkedIn profile, ask your network
- Intuition – are there are any red flags and can you resolve them
- Selection – are they the right fit for you
- Control/Choices – how much control do you have about your resume, the application process, are you making informed choices
- Questions – what questions are you not asking? Do you have all the information you need? If not, then ask more.

Some of those questions can be:
- Do you work with the client exclusively?
- Are you on their preferred supplier list?
- Have you worked with them before?
- What is the hiring process?
- Do you know why they are hiring?
- How well do you know the hiring team?
- Can you find out any more information?
- Are you retained by the employer?

The more 'No's you get to the above questions, the more likely they are not a close partner of the employer. You cannot dismiss them just yet as they could just be working with a new client and may still be building trust with the employer. Dig a little deeper and see if the recruiter is transparent with you about their relationship. If they provide decent information, you are well placed to decide if you are on the right track and want to work with them.

7.7 MANAGING YOUR DATA AND PRIVACY

The golden rule for jobseekers is simple: this is your career, so treat the job search process with the utmost respect and don't be cavalier with how you mange your resume and personal information.

When working with a recruitment company, I always suggest that before you submit your resume via their website or by email that you call first and ask what they will do with it. With the recent changes to privacy laws, especially GDPR in Europe, you are the owner of your data.

If you cannot get a response, by phone or by email, with how they will manage your data, then be careful about taking it any further. I prefer an email reply as you have a written record of how they will manage your data.

Don't be fooled by recruiters who say: "We are so busy we just don't have time to ask for your consent every time a job comes up so please just provide blanket consent." For me that is a red flag, a line in the sand that you should not cross, as you will have no idea where they will send your resume. Ask yourself what other information they may withhold from you.

It is much easier if they state on their website that they will only use your data for helping you find a job and they will not pass it on to anyone without your express permission. That means they must contact you and get your authority before they send your resume or bio to each and every client. It is your absolute right both to provide and withhold consent on how your data is used. This protects you from having your resume and name sent to employers without your knowledge.

Now that you have all the information to apply for jobs and be in the top 1% of applicants, I recommend reading Part 8 before you take that next step. This section details three case studies, packed with analysis and pro tips. I know you will find something useful in each, so read them and then consider your applications.

PART 8:
CASE STUDIES—PERMANENT JOBS

Up to now, we have explored the world of recruitment and how to plan your job search. The following case studies build on this information with illustrative and practical tips to further support you.

I address some 'pro tips' more than once to reinforce the message. If this is the first section of the book you read, then I recommend reading Part 5 as well which covers managing your LinkedIn profile as part of your job search. In addition, I have included some brief chapters in Part 10 answering some of the questions most asked by jobseekers.

These case studies are based on real examples I have seen throughout my career. I hope to show you how the recruitment process works from the perspective of the employer and their HR team, the recruiter and the candidates. They are detailed and address questions I am asked on a day-to-day basis.

I recommend you read all the case studies and take what applies to and resonates with you. Two examples are for permanent jobs and one is for a contract role.

Each case study comes with analysis, tips and suggestions for each situation as it arises and how it may apply to you. With these in mind, you can navigate most scenarios you face in your job search.

8.1 CASE STUDY 1: MAKING SPECULATIVE APPLICATIONS

8.1.1. BIG LAW AND CASSIE STONE

Cassie Stone is a lawyer in a large US law firm in London. She works long hours for an unforgiving boss, but she loves her work and has a very clear mission; she will wait five years and then she will set up her own business in the world of 'law tech'. Cassie is also learning to write code which means she has little spare time. She is naturally trusting and diligent about running her life. She has just bought her first home and was careful not to over extend herself financially, making sure that, should interest rates rise, she has plenty of room to cover increases in her mortgage repayments.

In short, Cassie expects people to be honest. She is one of the top performers at her firm and known for managing complex problems well. She also has a knack for managing client relationships when her boss, who is like a bull in a china shop, explodes in another fit of anger. She often has to pick up the pieces caused by his oversized ego.

Cassie is well aware that if she wants to set up her own technology business, then she should get some exposure to working in a technology company or another law tech business, so she decides to start the job search process now.

She has a strong group of friends, so she asks her network for any suggestions for good recruiters. She quickly finds there is a great recruiter called Ruby that some of her friends have used. Ruby used to work for a well-known tech company but left to set up her own recruitment business specialising in high growth tech companies. She has an excellent track record and is also a friend of one of Cassie's yoga buddies, Morgan.

Having thought about how to approach her job search, Cassie gives Ruby a call on Monday morning. She knows that only a few roles are advertised at companies she would like to work for, so she also changes her privacy settings in LinkedIn to "Let recruiters know you are looking".

"Hi Ruby, its Cassie Stone calling. I work at Big Law and our friend Morgan suggested I call you."

"Thanks Cassie. Yes, Morgan mentioned you might call. How can I help you?"

Cassie can hear typing in the background and just as she is about to ask if she should call back later, Ruby says "OK, I've just found you on LinkedIn and sent you a connection request." Cassie hears a ping on her phone and sure enough, a notification has just popped up on her screen. She accepts.

Cassie has been rehearsing her elevator pitch and reels off the latest version of her career story.

"I've been with Big Law for five years now as a technology lawyer and I'm looking for a change. I really want to work for a tech company and have started taking a coding course at General Assembly. Ideally, I'd love to work for myself in a few years, but I need some exposure away from traditional law firms."

"OK, my clients will only recruit you at the moment as a lawyer but, if you position yourself well, you may be able to move into the business side. How long are you prepared to commit to your next role for?"

"I think I'll need to gain at least three years' experience, though I hope it will be my last corporate job."

"OK, thanks for your honesty, Cassie. If you had said anything less, I would be more hesitant to help you as most of my clients don't want job-hoppers. Knowing so many leave to do what you want to do, they have careful screening processes."

"Ruby, I know that you work for technology companies but do you have any experience of placing lawyers into your clients?"

"Actually, yes. As these companies grow, they are building out their legal, compliance and regulatory teams, especially because of GDPR in Europe and protecting their software from infringement. But they don't hire very often. If you want a more mainstream role, we can discuss those as there are definitely more opportunities."

"Thanks, Ruby. At the moment I would like to keep it to a fairly narrow field around some high growth tech companies such as Alltech where I hear the culture is really progressive and dynamic. Do you have any relationships there?"

"Yes, but I'll need to ask you a few questions."

"Sure."

"I see you went to Bristol University and then you attended a short course at Harvard which is excellent. What were your grades?"

"I graduated with a 1st class Honours in Law and was offered a few training contracts but I went with Big Law and been there ever since."

"Who is your supervising partner?"

"Most of my work is with Jemma Stone but I also work for Mark Cage."

"Brilliant. Jemma has an excellent reputation and close links to Google, Alltech and IBM. I also know Mark and his moods, but he is a great lawyer."

"Yes", laughs Cassie nervously, "that is very true."

"How much are you earning?" Cassie hesitates and asks why. Ruby explains that the salary she earns now is not that relevant to what she will earn elsewhere and it is more to set a financial expectation.

"Around £150,000 but with a £25,000 bonus."

"OK, that is within reach for our clients but at the moment I don't have any roles for you.

"Have you applied anywhere else or spoken to any other recruiters?"

"No, not at this stage."

"OK, please send me a copy of your resume if you have one and I will be in touch when something turns up. Of course, I should add that we won't send it anywhere until we talk again and there is a job which both suits you and you want to apply for. Don't worry; I'll confirm this all in an email."

"Great, thanks Ruby."

Takeaway—asking a recruiter to help with your job search

- Cassie found Ruby through a friend; a great place to start. Always ask your network first.
- Remember that 99% of recruiters use LinkedIn and the first thing they do is search for you. Update your resume and LinkedIn profile before you approach any recruiters if you are ready to start your job search now.
- Cassie and Ruby were both transparent about what they wanted and Ruby was clear about whether she could help.
- Ruby sounded as if she understood her market well and has great experience in her niche.
- Ruby explains that even though she would like to see a copy of Cassie's resume, she will not send it out without Cassie's consent. This is key to establishing how much control you retain over your resume and the recruitment process. An email confirming this is perfect as you now have a written record.

Two weeks later Cassie receives an unsolicited message on LinkedIn from a recruiter called Toby.

"Hi Cassie, I am a head hunter with TC Consultants and have a few clients interested in seeing your resume. Your LinkedIn profile is excellent and the market is active for lawyers with your skills. Call me if you want to talk. My phone number is 0123 456 789."

Cassie doesn't think it can do any harm and she has heard nothing back from Ruby, so she calls Toby.

"Thanks for calling, Cassie. I really think I can help you. What are you looking for?"

"Well, ideally I don't want to work in practice anymore but would prefer to look at in-house roles in tech companies."

"OK, that's fine. I have very good contacts within the law departments. If you send me your resume, I will ask some of my clients if they want to talk, though I know they will as you have an amazing background. They will love you. Sorry I have to take another call but email me your resume and I will be in touch again soon."

They exchange email addresses. Cassie fires off her resume and gets back to work.

Takeaway—managing unsolicited messages from recruiters

- Cassie did not carry out any research before calling Toby, but he approached her and he appears to be genuine.
- She sends her resume with no knowledge of what Toby will do with it.
- Toby says he will talk to some of his clients. Does this mean anonymously, or will he send Cassie's resume anyway?
- Ideally Cassie should not send her resume through until she has spoken to Toby again.
- The less information you obtain about the recruiter and their reputation, the more difficulty you can find yourself in. The more information you get, the better prepared you are to decide if they can genuinely help you. At this stage, we don't know whether Toby is a good recruiter. Following the RISCQ formula helps:
  - Research: Gather information, look at their website, social media, LinkedIn profile and ask your network.

- Intuition: Are there are any red flags and can you resolve them?
- Selection: Are they the right fit for you?
- Control/Choices: How much control do you have about your resume, the application process and making informed choices?
- Questions: What questions are you not asking and do you have all the information you need? If not, then get more.

Some of these questions can be:

- Asking how long they have worked as a consultant, especially if there is little information on their website.
- Asking about their LinkedIn profile. It may be a new business they are still building, so may not reflect their ability to help you, i.e. they may have been working for an employer and now are working for themselves or they may be new to recruitment.
- Asking about their client relationships: What type of clients do you work for? Who will you talk to? How well do you know them? How long have you worked for them?
- Asking about their process: Are you retained by your clients? Do you work exclusively on roles? (Review Part 2 to understand what retained and exclusive mean.) How is my data managed?

- Many excellent recruiters work on their own, as well as in large recruitment companies. Don't let the size of the recruitment business determine how good you think they are. In most cases, it depends on the skills and professionalism of the individual recruiter. I recommend getting to know some of the recruiters in the independent boutiques; many of them have great reputations across their industries.

Another two weeks pass by. Cassie has been flat out at work. She has heard nothing back from Toby but presumes he is just waiting to hear from his clients. Late on Thursday evening she gets a call from Ruby.

"Hi Cassie, apologies for not talking to you in a while. However, I've just had an email from Alltech and they are looking for a tech lawyer. I think your profile is perfect for them. I am due to talk to them tomorrow and I would love to have a chat to them about you. At this stage I won't mention you by name but will give enough for them to see how well qualified you are. Is that OK with you?"

"Thanks, Ruby. That would be great. Are you sure they won't know who I am? We work closely with them and it would be awkward if they knew who I was. I would hate my manager to find out."

"Don't worry, Cassie. We do this all the time. I promise they will not know who you are. I will get back to you tomorrow afternoon with their feedback. Is that OK with you?"

Against the clatter of typing, Cassie says that will be fine. Excited, she sets off for a few drinks with some work friends, celebrating in advance what could be her dream job.

Just after lunch the following day, Ruby calls back and tells Cassie that based on the information Ruby gave her, Alltech would love to meet her.

Ruby realises Cassie is a little nervous and explains: "We would only put you forward if we thought you had a real chance of securing the role. They trust us and know that any candidates we introduce will be more than capable of being successful with them."

Cassie remains concerned about her boss Mark finding out as they have a deal about to start. Ruby reassures her they are discreet and the process will be safe. Cassie agrees to put her resume forward and Ruby promises to be back in touch early the following week.

Sitting at home on Friday afternoon, Ruby is trying to get everything cleared from her diary so she can start on Monday without a backlog. Her mobile phone chirps and she recognises Judith's number, the Talent Acquisition lead of Alltech. That was quick, she thinks with a smile.

As soon as Judith starts talking Ruby knows that something is wrong and her hearts skips a beat; Cassie would be a great help for her quarterly KPI's and her fee is almost £50,000.

"Ruby, something worrying has come up with Cassie Stone. I know that we've worked together for years, but I think you need to know that we've already received Cassie's resume from TC Consultants. To be honest, I don't know them, but they put her application in first. We want to interview her and she looks perfect but I can't do it through you at the moment."

"Are they a preferred agency, Judith? I haven't heard of them though new ones pop up every day. How come they even managed to submit her resume? I thought this role was off the grid."

"To be honest, I don't know either, but he made a general application on her behalf. What I need for you to do is send me any correspondence you have with Cassie, including her consent for you to act and we will see where we get to. However, at the moment I cannot accept your introduction."

Not another one, thinks Ruby. That is all I need. Who on earth is Toby from TC Consultants? A quick LinkedIn search tells her that, like many others, he has hopped around a few smaller agencies before setting up on his own.

Thankfully, Ruby makes excellent notes in her head hunting CRM and also logs all calls and emails. She can easily print them off and they are time and date stamped.

She calls Cassie, who explains that she did not give Toby permission to disclose her details and he was only to have an anonymous call. Cassie agrees to confirm that in writing and fires off an email to Ruby, as well as one to Toby asking what he is doing.

Toby calls her saying: "What is all the fuss about? I said I knew people and I got you an interview. What more do you want?"

Cassie reiterates that while she is grateful for the interview, she never suggested that he had her permission to float her resume around and she had told him how sensitive it was with her employer.

He replies: "Why does that matter? The interview is all that counts."

With a long sigh, Cassie looks up from her desk. Her boss Mark has just walked in with a scowl on his face. He is never in the best of moods but now his face is deep scarlet.

"I'll call you back," she says tightly.

"Cassie, I just had a call from Jim Watts at Alltech and he tells me they have your resume. What are you playing at? We have a huge deal about to start and you are going to leave? I am seriously unimpressed."

He slams the door and walks out. She calls Ruby and explains what just happened.

"Cassie, I am so sorry. This should never happen. But it's such a small world. People talk. It is wrong at every level, but they still do it."

"What can he do, Ruby?"

"Well in reality, Cassie, not much. Yes, he can be a pain with your reference. And yes, he can put in a bad word, although unlikely. You can always ask Jemma for a reference instead. I am more worried about what happens if you don't get the role and stay at Big Law. He can make your life very hard. Leave it with me. I will speak to Judith in the talent team and we will sort it out. Thanks for your email, by the way. I've already forwarded it to them."

It was now 5.45pm and there was no reply from Judith. Ruby lets Cassie know she will have to wait until Monday, though she suggests Cassie let Toby know that she did not give him permission to send her resume out. She also recommends Cassie asks Toby to withdraw her application from Alltech.

Cassie fires off another email to Toby and endures an uncomfortable weekend, mostly at work; her boss dumped a stack of work on her desk as she was about to walk out the door on Friday evening.

She thought about just walking anyway and leaving him to stew, but knew that would be worse. By Monday, she was exhausted and had a splitting headache. A call from Ruby would help.

"Good news, Cassie. You've dodged an almighty bullet for now. Alltech still want to see you and you can interview through us. It turns out that our friend Toby is drinking buddies with Jim Watts' junior and that is how your resume ended up in their systems.

"Jim Watts was mortified and apologises for telling your boss. He thought he knew already, as that is what Toby had told his friend. Needless to say, Toby won't be working with them again in a hurry."

"Oh no, Ruby," Cassie shrieks. While on the phone with Ruby, she has opened an email from Toby with a list of 23 potential employers he has sent her resume to. Many of them are clients and a few she would never want to work for.

"What do I do now?"

"Well, let's focus on Alltech first. But this is why we tell people to manage their resume carefully."

After a four-week interview process, Alltech hires Cassie.

Cassie asked Toby to withdraw her application from all 23 other potential employers.

8.1.2 CASE STUDY 1 ANALYSIS

The lessons learned are obvious. There is a sizeable difference between recruiters who want to work with you and those whose mission it is to make quick money, often at your expense.

I cannot foresee whether Cassie's experience with Toby will happen to you, but with the proliferation of recruiters, you will get bad ones. They can be in any recruitment business, however reputable you may think they are; I see this often with my clients.

If this happens to you, manage the situation as follows:

- Ask for a list of all the companies the recruiter has sent your resume to.
- Withdraw your application from those employers and request the other recruiter to manage your application process for you.
- Consider the companies that received your resume. Contact them and withdraw your application advising the reason why, unless you have already accepted an offer elsewhere, or it is an employer you would never approach anyway.
- Notify the recruiter by email that you are ceasing to work with them and that they do not have and have never had your consent to submit your resume.
- Request the recruiter remove all of your data and personal information from their database.
- Email the recruiter who you do want to work with confirming that you have not given your consent for anyone else to submit your resume and they are the only authorised agency to act on your behalf.

Pro Tips—finding and working with good recruiters

The best recruiters work in a niche/sector/industry they know well. Many have real world career experience in those sectors, but others have also learned it. Your recruiter need not be an expert in their sector, but it helps. The key is their relationships and how well their clients trust them.

If a recruiter approaches you through LinkedIn, you are not under any obligation to reply. Many people worry about being discourteous. If they send you a message which appears genuine, about jobs you are interested in, then check out their LinkedIn profile and their website if they have one. Only then reply and arrange to talk. Don't just send out your resume. If the message is spam and/or generic, delete it or ignore it.

Takeaway–Making speculative applications

In the case of Cassie Stone and Toby from TC Consultants, Toby made a speculative application to Alltech. If a recruiter suggests making a speculative application, ask them to do so anonymously first, as Ruby did with Cassie Stone. Based on the feedback they receive from the employer, they can let you, the jobseeker, decide how to proceed.

I remember when a candidate contacted me and wanted to work in SE Asia. They had very specific experience, usually in high demand, but the market was quiet. A few other recruiters had sent this candidate's resume out to many employers without success. I knew all the hiring managers and knew they were not hiring. Even though this candidate's resume had been sent out to more than 20 employers by other recruiters, I continued to work with them as I had a client in Tokyo who I knew may be interested. There was only a small chance of success, but the client was proactive and they hired my candidate.

In this case, the candidate landed the job they wanted after a lengthy process where their resume was sent out to many prospective employers who all said no. I cannot comment on whether the candidate agreed to that but the point is twofold. First, they landed the job, so they may not have cared and second, never give up because when you find the recruiters who understand their market they will work for you.

8.2 CASE STUDY 2: GETTING HEAD-HUNTED AND WORKING WITH RETAINED RECRUITERS

8.2.1 MEDIACO

This case study highlights:
- The roles that the employer, including the line manager and talent acquisition team, play in the recruitment process
- The pressures the employer faces
- How that pressure impacts the recruiters and ultimately you, the jobseeker

Variations of this example play out around the world daily. Your perspective will change based on which candidate you are and how you perceive the interaction between the recruiters and the employer.

New York based MediaCo are rolling out a new, rapidly expanding project, so they have given Gina, the newly promoted Head of Talent Acquisition, a mandate to hire five graphic designers.

Sarah Volk runs a well-known boutique digital recruitment agency with a stellar reputation, called SHV, and has worked with MediaCo for several years.

MediaCo gives the mandate to SHV, one of their preferred suppliers, exclusively for 30 days. No other recruitment agencies can submit candidates during this time.

SHV charges 20% of the candidate's first year salary, which is on average $120,000. Sarah's agency fees will be around $120,000 for five successful placements.

Gina has been clear that the department head she is recruiting on behalf of, Scott, has very definite views on the type of person he wants to hire. They must come from a pre-selected list of employers, though he might entertain someone outside the list if their work is unique. Scott is also not a fan of recruiters and sees little value in what they can offer. He thinks he can do it himself, but every time he is involved with direct recruitment it has ended badly. Gina has worked hard to bring him round to using external agencies.

Insights

From an outsider's point of view we have little insight into the background or pressure that both Gina and Sarah face. But we know Gina has recently been promoted to her role while this is a significant fee for Sarah's business.

MediaCo are one of Sarah's larger clients in a competitive market. It is the first time her agency has been given an exclusive mandate with them which she worked hard to win.

Sarah has also just hired a new consultant, Jo, and is going to hand this piece of work to her. Jo is an experienced consultant but has never worked with MediaCo, though she knows all of their competitors well.

There are many more variables I could add in or change. Jo could be a new consultant that Sarah is training. Jo could be a consultant who is buying a house and needs the commission to top up her deposit, so is more financially driven than usual. All these factors can play into your experience with managing the application process and your perception of whether SHV are doing a great job. You could be one of the five candidates who happily secure a job or you could miss out at the last interview and develop a negative perception of SHV.

As a jobseeker, all you care about is a transparent process where you are treated with respect and given a fair chance to secure the role.

We will see four candidates go through the process with SHV, all with differing outcomes. You will see each of their perspectives based on how they are treated. These perspectives feed back into the wider prevailing sentiment of the recruitment industry, or at least what you might see on social media. Just remember that every day tens of thousands of people are being offered new jobs and are excited to be starting a new role.

Jo starts the recruitment process. This involves searching SHV's internal database of candidates and asking the research team to build a target list based on the list of employers that Gina has suggested. Due to the time constraints, MediaCo also agrees to pay for a job ad on LinkedIn.

We will track the progress of four of the candidates: Ricardo, Neroli, Samantha and Charlie.

Ricardo works for a rival competitor to MediaCo and is already on SHV's database, although no-one has spoken to him before.

Neroli has been an independent graphic designer for well over a decade and, while she has worked on large accounts and trained at Apple, she has freelanced for the six years since the birth of her first child. Her client list is excellent.

Samantha works for another major competitor of MediaCo and has a near perfect background for the role but was a little evasive during the screening calls.

Charlie works for Agency1, a competitor of MediaCo and has recent digital design experience for production companies. He also works for a well-known woman in the industry.

Both Neroli and Charlie apply for the role through the LinkedIn ad while Samantha is a referral.

The research team at SHV contact Ricardo and book him in for an appointment to see Jo the following week.

Week 1:

Yolinda runs the research team and has a catch up with Jo to discuss the candidates at the end of the first week.

"So how is our shortlist going, Yolinda?"

"Well, we've had over 200 applications to date and with the background that MediaCo want there are only 12 that I think we should bring in for an interview with you."

They talk a little more and the list grows to 14 as they both feel they need to make sure they don't miss anyone, especially as the job will go to the market in less than 3 weeks.

Weeks 2—3:

Jo meets all 14 candidates over the course of the next two weeks. All of them consent to being put forward to the client. Yolinda has explained to each of them that the process will take about four to six weeks from the first interview until a formal offer, and it will be a two-step interview process with a design task involved. Jo has another session with Yolinda on Friday morning telling her:

"I need to call Gina later today to give her an update as Scott is being his usual self and causing a few problems. Having seen all of them, I think we have a shortlist of ten that would work well for Gina and I want to get their resumes across to her on Monday."

Jo highlights four in particular and asks Yolinda for her thoughts.

"Ricardo seems to be the stand out candidate though he was a head hunt call. While interested, he is being well looked after and enjoys his work. The only reason he would move is for the work MediaCo are getting from Unity Pictures. What do you think?"

"Yes, I think he will leave but the interview process will be critical as he is still on the fence a bit. I know MediaCo are great at interviewing and for all of Scott's weirdness he is still excellent and looks after his team really well. He just doesn't like anyone else interfering."

"OK, Charlie and Samantha also seem to be a good fit for them. MediaCo are looking for multiple roles and Charlie works for Agency1 which is one of their peers. His background is really strong."

"What about Neroli?" asks Yolinda.

Jo is silent for a while, remembering her conversation the previous week with Gina that she could consider a left–of–centre candidate, an outlier, even if unlikely.

"To be honest, I like her and she has some fantastic experience. Not just her training at Apple, but some of her freelance work is exceptional and her client list is stellar. Have you seen her digital folio? It's beautiful. Personally, I trust her well enough to include her in the list, but I need to talk to Gina first. They've never been keen on flexible working and

Neroli hasn't worked for a corporate for a long time. Why does she want a full-time permanent role now?"

"Pretty simple; her daughter is at school now and she wants to expand her folio again and get involved in projects for longer, see the entire project through not just pieces of it. Also, having a constant salary would suit her better now."

"OK, let me run it by Gina."

Later that day, Jo calls Gina and talks her through the shortlist. Unfortunately Gina is clear that Neroli, although she sounds excellent, will not fit in with Scott. He has been clear about his thoughts on paying fees for someone like this candidate. Jo did not disclose Neroli's name or anything that can identify her. Her privacy has not been compromised.

Rather than let her wait over the weekend, Jo calls Neroli and explains why she cannot put her forward.

Takeaway—applying early, managing your privacy and being the 'outlier':

- *Don't wait too long to apply for a role. In this example, they make the shortlist at the end of the first week of advertising. Even though they may advertise the job for 30 days, there is no guarantee they will wait that long before hiring someone.*

- *The research team has notified all the candidates of the timeframe for the process. If the recruiter does not tell you, ask how long the process will be. You need to find out if you will be around for the interviews, especially if you have any holidays planned.*

- *All resumes are submitted with the express consent of the candidates.*

- *Even though the recruiter has a great relationship with the client, she still cannot persuade them to interview Neroli. She does not tick all the right boxes, though she could do the role easily.*

- *More often than not you may be the 'Neroli'. The recruiter may not put you forward but will explain why. It is also true that the recruiter may not inform you after your application is rejected. This has happened to me. Yes, it can be frustrating. Just make a mental note if you consider working with this recruiter again, but don't be precious. Develop a thick skin when working with recruiters until you find the ones who want to work with you. Many times I have coached jobseekers where the recruiter was distant at first but comes back to them, even months later, with a job that they get hired for.*

Week 4:

All the resumes are submitted to Gina at MediaCo and she promises to let Jo know by the end of the week whom they want to interview. Friday afternoon comes along and Jo has heard nothing further.

At 5.30 pm Jo is still working, trying to clear her desk for the weekend when her phone rings.

"Hi, it's Jo. How can I help?"

"Hi Jo. It's Samantha. I was wondering what was happening with my application to MediaCo. Is there any news yet?"

"You're lucky to catch me, Samantha. I was heading out of the door. And no, I haven't heard anything. They promised us some feedback today, but I'll call them on Monday. They haven't commented on anyone yet, so you are still in the game. If you don't hear from me, it is only because there's no news."

"Thanks, Jo. It's just that I had an interview with Scanlan this week which came out of the blue through another recruitment agency and they want to meet again next week. They seem really keen, but I would love to meet MediaCo. What do you think I should do?"

Samantha was one of the 'bankers' (recruitment speak for definite hires) that Jo had highlighted for the role, so Jo's heart sank when she heard this. She suggests Samantha continue with Scanlan but tries to persuade her to defer her next interview until the week after to buy some time for MediaCo. Jo reassures her that they can move fast if they need to, bearing in mind they are hiring for multiple roles.

Samantha also clarifies that she does not want MediaCo to find out about the Scanlan opportunity which presents another headache for Jo.

Before Jo walks out of the door, her mobile rings. Sarah has just got off a plane from Los Angeles and wants an update on MediaCo.

Week 5:

Jo gets an email from Gina on Sunday afternoon confirming they want to interview ten candidates. Gina says it was a stretch to get Scott to agree and Jo should arrange with her team on Monday to set up the interviews for this week.

Rather than calling each one, Jo arranges for Yolinda to explain the next steps via email. She also sends out a guide to interviews, explaining how to answer a few standard questions, as well as information about the interviewers.

The team set up the interviews, which all go ahead. Gina promises more feedback by the end of the following week as Scott is on holiday.

Week 6:

On Thursday, Jo calls Gina for an update and receives the green light for eight of the candidates to proceed to the next stage, which is to complete a design task by the end of the following week.

Samantha, Charlie and Ricardo are included.

Yolinda makes the calls to the two rejected candidates and explains why.

Samantha interviews at Scanlan and, while waiting for feedback, agrees to go ahead with the design task.

Jo reassures Samantha that until she accepts an unconditional offer, she should continue the process with MediaCo.

> *Takeaway—interviewing with multiple employers:*
>
> - *You do not need to inform a potential employer that you are interviewing with another company. It is your choice. Some employers will ask if you are talking to anyone else and others will not. The assumption is that if you are talking to them, you are talking to others. If you are concerned that you are not being truthful, then you can simply say that you are considering a few opportunities.*
>
> - *Whether you have been head hunted by a recruiter or applied for a job through multiple recruiters, remember that they all have differing levels of transparency. They will apply differing levels of pressure to you to complete the interview process and accept the*

> *job their company has introduced to you. They are all financially motivated for you to land the job which pays them.*
>
> - *Some employers are more flexible regarding interview dates, gathering referees and signing the offer letter and contract. It depends on the urgency to fill that role, i.e. if it is an interim or contract role then if you delay, you may miss out.*
>
> - *The internal talent acquisition teams, HR teams and line manager will note how easy or hard you were to manage through the interviewing process, which can translate into positive or negative expectations of you when you start.*

Week 7:

It's Friday afternoon and Jo's mobile phone buzzes. She recognises Gina's number.

"Hi Gina, how did the candidates go with the design task?"

"They did well, Jo. There are six that we want to take to final interview but Scott has decided that due to the pressure he is getting from his clients he wants to shorten the interview process and complete it all next week.

"He really likes the look of Samantha, Charlie and Ricardo so fingers crossed for them. Since Scott has said we'll make offers by this time next week or at the latest the Monday following, is there anything else we need to be aware of? Are any interviewing elsewhere?"

Jo is well aware that Samantha is under pressure with Scanlan, but also understands that Samantha does not want MediaCo to know.

"As you can expect, several are talking to other companies but at this stage everyone feels that their preference is for MediaCo. Concluding the process next week will take the pressure off. We can talk more about that when you make offers."

"OK, thanks, Jo. I get the picture and we'll move as fast as we can. Does anyone have any issues interviewing next week?"

"I think we're in luck as everyone is around, though remember that Iqbal is based in Boston. Do you want to see him in person or is video ok?"

"I think we need to see him in person. Is that going to be a problem?"

"Not sure as it is short notice, but let me call and ask him and I'll get back to you."

"OK. Oh, and before I go, we will now only be recruiting four roles as Scott has just hired someone totally left-of-centre through one of his own contacts. You know what he can be like. I can see why he liked her, though she has been freelancing for years, much like the candidate we discussed. I said no before, as Scott was very specific about this. But, he didn't have to pay any recruiters, so it was a double win for him.

"Someone from the team will email you some interview times. You should get them in the next 15 minutes. If you don't, then call me as I know we're pushed for time."

Jo just saw one of her fees evaporate and sighed. She thought of Neroli immediately and made a mental note to call her.

Two hours later, Yolinda's team have frantically arranged the interviews for next week.

Jo is about to send Gina an email saying everyone is organised, including Iqbal, who is coming to New York for a meeting anyway, which is lucky.

Jo's phone chirps. It is Neroli.

"Hi Neroli, that's good timing as I had a note to call you to check in."

"Well, Jo, you will not believe this, but I just signed a contract with MediaCo. I know the HR team said they would not look at me and I appreciate all your support. But it turns out one of my clients knew Scott and they suggested he call me as they knew I was looking for a permanent role. I know he can be a little weird but his team love him and it was the perfect opportunity. He knows my work and best of all I can work from home two days a week."

"That is great, Neroli. Funnily enough, Gina did tell me that Scott had made a hire and it sounded just like you. Many congratulations. When do you start?"

"In two weeks. By the way I also wanted to give you a heads up as having met Scott a couple of times, he has some strong opinions. He was picking my brains to see if I knew of anyone else who may fit in. He definitely does not like recruiters.

"I have a friend who has been at Agency1 for ages and would consider MediaCo as they want to move into the digital motion graphic space. Scott was curious as he knows they have high quality work and training but apparently he had a big falling out recently with Jenny Rock. They worked together on a project and he is convinced that her team copied his work and called it their own. He won't touch anyone from her team.

"Anyway, I just wanted to call and say thanks for supporting me."

She rang off. Jo sat there in disbelief. Not only had Scott hired Neroli for free and there was nothing she could do about it, but she also knew Charlie worked for Jenny and that sounded ominous for him. However, she also knew Scott had agreed to interview him, so she needed to talk to Charlie about his interview prep.

Week 8: The Interviews

Yolinda sent out more interview guides to all the candidates on Friday and Jo booked in some interview prep for all the candidates on Monday.

Takeaway—interview preparation

- *Ask your recruiter if they have an interview guide. Larger volume recruitment companies and specialist boutiques often have reference guides to help with commonly asked interview questions like the weakness question, salary questions and behavioural questions. If they don't, then there are lots of examples on Google.*

- *Ask your recruiter for some interview preparation. Do they know the interviewing panel and the typical questions they ask? What kind of approach do they take? Your recruiter may not know this information if their client is new to them. However, your recruiter can ask the HR or talent acquisition liaison prior to the interview. It also depends on how engaged the internal recruiter is with the department or hiring manager; they can only pass on as much information as they themselves obtain. Each employer and business unit will be different, but you can still ask the questions.*

Jo talks to Charlie about Scott's view of his boss, Jenny. She explains that Scott knows Charlie has worked for Jenny's team, because it is on his resume, but he is still being interviewed which is positive. Charlie also relays to Jo that the deal Scott and Jenny worked on together, which led to their falling out, did not involve him. This may be enough to convince Scott that Charlie was not part of the 'betrayal' as Scott calls it. Jo suggests that Charlie focuses on his other achievements and client work not involving Jenny.

The interviews happen on Wednesday and Thursday. Jo calls the candidates to get their feedback. Charlie is the one she is most concerned about given Scott's views of his boss, but Charlie indicates that Scott was not concerned once he realised that Charlie had not been involved in the deal. Scott respects Jenny's work, if not her as a person.

Samantha also has a good interview but is under increasing pressure from the other recruiter as she has received an offer from Scanlan. They give her a deadline of Friday this week to accept. Samantha says Scott asked if she was talking to anyone else. She took Jo's earlier advice about being transparent now that she has an offer. Samantha said she was under offer, but she prefers to work for MediaCo.

Jo explains to Samantha that if an offer does not come through tomorrow, she can always ask Scanlan for a few more days.

Friday of Week 8:

Jo receives an email from Gina with offer letters for Samantha, Charlie, Ricardo and two others. In the end, Scott decides to make five offers. Gina has permission to hire all five but knows they may not all accept.

Gina also mentioned that Scott was fine with Charlie's experience, especially since he had not worked on the 'betrayal' deal.

Jo has overcome the first hurdle. Now her expertise really has to kick in to ensure she gets the offers accepted. She knows from previous experience that not all candidates are transparent about other opportunities. They can get counteroffers from their current employers and sometimes they just don't like the firm they interviewed with or the people they will report into.

Jo manages to get all five offers accepted.

Samantha, Charlie and Ricardo are all happy with their offers, but what if one of them had not received an offer? Would their perspective of the recruitment process change?

I have highlighted the challenges that recruiters and hiring teams face. You are protected from much of what goes on behind the scenes. You can see the amount of work put into securing you an offer and that these recruiters behave with integrity. However, if you had been a candidate rejected at the beginning, or after the first interview, would that view have changed? It is entirely personal. Samantha, Charlie, Ricardo and even Neroli may well recommend Jo and Sarah to their friends whereas others may not.

Takeaway—managing expectations, applying for multiple roles across sectors

- *I can honestly say from fifteen years as a head hunter, it was always easier to manage both a candidate and client's expectations if you are completely transparent all the way through the recruitment process.*

If you are a strong candidate and you build a good relationship with your recruiters, then it helps everyone if you are honest and make a full disclosure. Of course, it is always your decision how you want to manage your process and your private information. Your choice, you decide.

- *If you are looking at multiple roles but with different sectors, i.e. you are in career transition and are not sure which direction you should take, I would advise against disclosing too much information to either a recruiter or internal talent teams. Recruiters may weigh their chances of making money from placing you with how many opportunities you are pursuing elsewhere. They may decide you are unpredictable and decline to work with you or invest little time in you, though the more financially driven ones may take a different view. Similarly, internal talent teams may also think you are indecisive and not committed to them or their industry and you may move on quickly. This is more likely for a permanent role than a short term contract where you will leave anyway (unless they are looking to make that contract permanent). Weigh up the situation and be pragmatic about what you say and whom you tell.*

8.2.2 CASE STUDY 2 ANALYSIS

How to manage multiple offers

The advice from recruiters about whether to disclose information relating to offers or interviews elsewhere varies. It depends on your personal situation. You do not need to say anything specific.

If you are approached or head hunted, this may be the only role you are considering.

When you already have an offer secured and you want to use that as leverage for a role with another organisation, it is fine to negotiate with the second employer based on your offer. ***The key is to know your agenda:***

- Which employer do you really want to work for, money aside?
- Are you trying to get more money from the employer who made the first offer?
- Do you prefer to work for the second employer?
- Will you decide based on money, benefits or career progression?

Your negotiation strategy will depend on these factors. You don't want to blow your chances and you should get a sense through the interview process about where you stand.

Remember to compare apples with apples. For example, if you are looking at similar roles within the same industry at similar sized employers, then you may find there is more room to negotiate. However, if one is an enterprise player and the other a start-up, you have to work with what each can offer. There is nothing wrong with asking the questions, but I suggest you work out in advance what you really want and what you are prepared to accept.

When recruiters are managing the interview process, you may feel pressure from them to accept an offer for two reasons:

- Their client, and your future employer, may genuinely have the offer open for a fixed period before it lapses, meaning they need to plan themselves. If you do not accept their offer, they will make it to someone else. Remember that you can have an honest conversation with the employer, or you can ask the recruiter to do this for you, if you trust them to negotiate on your behalf. At least then you will have tried and the process will have come to its natural end.

- The recruiter wants to lock you in and get their fee to meet their commission target but there is no real time pressure.

If you have developed a transparent relationship with your recruiter, they will try to support you. Remember that it is always your decision about which offer to accept, not the recruiter's, so listen to your intuition. If something feels off, reflect on it as there is a reason your alarm bells are ringing.

When managing acceptance for a permanent role it is easier to delay as the employer may be hiring for a date several months away. They want to hire the candidate who is the best fit, so they are prepared to wait. They also know that depending on where the candidate works, notice periods differ; more senior candidates tend to have longer notice periods. If you are in the US, you may be subject to an 'at will' contract with no notice period, so your future employer may be trying to replace someone quickly. In the UK, Europe, and Australasia, notice periods can be both set and protected by law or in your contract.

8.2.3 THE ART OF NEGOTIATION

Your ability to negotiate the terms of an offer and apply leverage to multiple employers will change depending on whether:

- You already have a job
- You are contracting
- You are head hunted

If you want to change jobs or are out of work, it makes sense to explore several opportunities and if you interview well, then you can end up with more than one offer. It is up to you how much information about your other applications you want to share.

Sometimes sharing this information works in your favour, especially if you have secured an interview. You can use it as leverage to apply pressure on the other company to move their hiring process along. It all depends on how much of a competitive edge one employer believes they have.

I would not overthink this as it depends on your situation, the individual company and how much they want you.

When you already have a job, you can be more assertive with your negotiation style whereas if you are out of work you must balance getting a job with getting the right terms. If you are contracting and your contract is ending, you need to strike a similar balance.

You may be applying for jobs directly (not through recruiters) and interviewing with more than one potential employer. It can be overwhelming when deciding the best tactic and response for managing the interview process and answering the question: "Are you talking to anyone else?"

If you have no other interviews, then say: "I am not interviewing anywhere else." Alternatively, you can say: "I am looking at other opportunities and will let you know if they become more serious."

PART 9:

CASE STUDY—CONTRACTING

9.1 THE AGE OF THE FREELANCER

As the age of the freelance economy gains momentum, more people are looking to work on a contract basis and more employers are favouring fixed-term contracts over permanent contracts due to changing demands for their products and services.

Contract, interim and freelance work may become an essential part of your working life if you want to study, travel, care for children or elderly relatives, or build a side business. It means you can choose not to work all the time. Added bonuses are no notice periods to navigate and you are free to interview whenever a potential employer wants.

Before the Case Study, I wanted to highlight three key points of difference when looking for contract or consulting work compared to permanent roles:

- Speed
- Flexibility
- Preparation

The recruitment process for contract work is fast, which means a jobseeker can start work within a few days of the job being advertised. Be prepared to act quickly. Speed and preparation are your advantage. Have your resume ready, LinkedIn profile complete, and referees prepped. It does not matter whether you are a high earning executive or looking at casual contract work. The same principle applies; you need to be ready to move fast.

As I built my current business, I relied on consulting work which was not always guaranteed. However, I did not work with recruitment agencies as they provide contract work rather than consulting work. I could fill my diary with paid work as and when I chose, as long as the work was available.

> *Pro Tip: Flexibility and agility wins work*
>
> *If you want to explore consulting/contract work, you need to be flexible. I can tell you that the people who get the most work are prepared to bend over backwards to accommodate those who provide it. My diary was often full because I would go anywhere at short notice or take calls and meetings when others did not. Those opportunities often lead to other work and then your network of opportunity expands again.*

I believe that we create our own luck by hard work, kindness and by putting ourselves in the position for that luck to land. I remember consulting for one client where they kept delaying the work and cancelling at short notice, not due to poor operations but because their own client kept putting off the work. It became frustrating and I know some of my fellow consultants turned their work away as they only paid us for delivery and not for cancellations, but I persevered. Months later, when the work finally came through, serendipity also came calling and resulted in just under $1 million hitting my bank account shortly afterwards. If I had walked away from that work I would never have met the wonderful person, whom I was coaching through that consulting work, who helped to secure that life changing payment.

I have worked with numerous executives, some earning millions of dollars a year. I know that the turnaround time for a twelve month contract for a senior executive can be two weeks from the first phone call to an offer with a start date a week later. That is three weeks in total, including reference checks. Similarly, I coached a senior financial adviser through a career transition who accepted an interim role for a few months' work. All the interviews and background checks were completed within a week from the time of the recruiter's first phone call, with a start date four days later. Speed is of the essence and if you can move quickly and be flexible, then you stand an excellent chance of securing a job.

9.2 CASE STUDY: TAMMIE, A SENIOR EXECUTIVE ASSISTANT RETURNING TO WORK

Tammie is a Senior Executive Assistant who has worked with CEOs, Boards and other senior executives. She is returning to work after a two year break to care for her first child.

It has been a long time since she applied for a job. Her last role was as an EA to the CEO of a large company who she worked with for ten years after leaving school. She has little knowledge of current recruitment practices. She earned a good salary before but is not sure where to start looking for her next job. Thankfully, one of her old friends at her former employer now has her old job and can provide a bit of help, but Tammie hasn't spoken to her for a while and is nervous about asking for help.

Pro Tip: How to network to find work and overcoming fear of rejection

Asking for help is one of the hardest things for many people to do because of our natural human fears of rejection, being judged, lack of interest or lack of worth. I can promise you that most people like to help others. Ask yourself: "When was the last time someone asked me for help? What did I do?" I would imagine you saying "Well, yes, it happens quite often and as long as they are courteous I always help." So take that on board, pick up the phone or send a WhatsApp message or email and start networking.

A few years ago I was back in England after ten years living overseas, mainly in Australia and just before that in Bali, so my network was not as strong as it could have been. I was talking to my brother about my leadership consulting work and how I could expand that in London. He suggested calling someone I had known at primary school. I had not spoken to this person, Anthony, for 30 years and he was now one of the most well-known consultants in Europe, interviewing Prime Ministers and coaching heads of the United Nations on public speaking. I was daunted by this, but my memory of him was that he had always been kind and our paths had crossed a few times as adults but only in passing. I called him anyway and his advice and introductions led to two inter-related consulting projects.

I recommend listening to episode 99 of my podcast, Human Impact, where I talk to Dr David Burkus, a world authority on the science and practicality of networking and author of "Friend of a Friend". Also check out episode 105 with Bob Burg, best-selling author of "The Go Giver" series.

Tammie calls her friend and gets the number for Sunil, a recruiter her friend has spoken to a few times. Still a little anxious, Tammie calls Sunil though she is not too clear on what she wants.

"Sunil speaking. How can I help you?"

"Hi Sunil, my name is Tammie. My colleague, Meg, suggested I call you as I used to work in her position and I'm just coming back from maternity leave."

"Thanks, Tammie. How long did you work there?"

"Ten years. Ever since I left school. I worked my way up. I also have a diploma in office management which they sponsored me for."

Tammie hears tapping in the background. Sunil says he is looking at her LinkedIn profile and can see she has not updated it in a while. He asks for her resume which is also a little out of date. The last time she wrote a resume was five years ago when another recruiter called her about a role she decided against interviewing for.

"Well, Tammie, I'll need you to update your resume and LinkedIn profile. The way we write resumes is a little different now but we have some templates on our website that you can use as a basis for yours. I'll have a quick look at it when you've done it. Are you ready to start work now?

"Yes, but I'd like to work three to four days a week, preferably on a contract as I want to see how I go for the first six months. What sort of roles do you have?"

"Well, the first question is how much do you need to earn? And what type of work do you want to do? Going back to an EA role can be very time consuming. Realistically, your four days will be five, but we do have job share roles which come up for return-to-work mums, including things like top level receptionist roles.

"The thing is, Tammie, these roles come up and go quickly. Sometimes for short-term contract roles we have the person placed within a week, so you need to be ready with your resume, your LinkedIn profile and a start date.

"I do have a role which you'd be great for but they want to see resumes by the end of the week at the latest. Do you think you can manage that?"

Tammie says she will come back to him as she has not made any decisions yet. She carries out some job searches on LinkedIn and has conversations with a few recruiters. Only one offers as much help as Sunil but they all have the same key questions: what do you want, how much do you want, is your resume ready and can you start now?

None of them seem concerned about how long she wants to work for or what happens when the contract ends but they do all ask whether she would be prepared to extend her contract.

Tammie calls Sunil back a week later having spent some time with her friend Meg organising her resume and LinkedIn profile.

"Hi Tammie, well sadly that job has gone but there is another we are working on that may suit you even better. There are a couple of tweaks to your LinkedIn profile that you should make and your resume is pretty good, but I suggest more focus on your achievements around using and implementing technology, especially for this role. Aside from that it looks great. Are you ready to start? Have you applied elsewhere?"

Tammie keeps quiet as she has registered her resume with a few other agencies but has not yet heard back. Refer to Part 7 for information about registering your resume with recruiters.

She promises to get her resume back to Sunil by the end of the day. Sunil gets her permission to submit her resume to his client and within 36 hours Tammie is interviewing with Sunil's client, a large logistics business. It seems a good fit and they are flexible with working arrangements.

They offer Tammie the job, check her references and she is able to start in two weeks. Before she accepts she has another call with Sunil as she is unsure about what to do at the end of the contract, which is for six months ending at Christmas.

"To be honest, Tammie, there is normally plenty of work for someone with your skills, but the more flexibility you want around working hours, the fewer roles there will be. You need to work that out for yourself and your family.

"The contract ends at Christmas and the market will be quiet in January. See how the role goes. Maybe you can extend it for a month or two nearer the time."

"OK, that is great. And what if I decide to leave and take a few months off and then start work again?"

"As far as I'm concerned, and provided you give me plenty to time to find you other roles, it doesn't matter. All I ask is that you keep me informed of your plans and let me know well in advance what you want to do. This will be a great opportunity to see if you enjoy working in this type of role and whether it provides enough for you financially and supports your career goals and your family priorities."

Pro Tip: How to work best with contract recruiters

- *Contract recruiters can be extremely busy. They run multiple job mandates which they need to fill quickly, so always be prepared. In this case, Sunil was happy to help, but not all recruiters are so obliging, though this does not make them bad recruiters either.*

- *Sunil seems to do his best for Tammie and he is one that she should keep on her list of recruiters to work with. I recommend finding three or four great recruiters to work with who will look out for you.*

- *In contract roles, be as clear as possible about the type of work that you are looking for and your availability. Contact the recruiters two to three months before your role ends and ask them what the usual timeframe is that works for their clients.*

- *Remember that the better you become at networking, the less you need to rely on recruiters.*

PART 10:
HARD QUESTIONS ANSWERED

10.1 WILL TAKING A CONTRACT ROLE OR AN INTERIM ROLE AFFECT MY CHANCES OF SECURING A PERMANENT JOB?

There are two key points to consider:

- How much do you need to earn to maintain your lifestyle?
- How will it impact your next job?

If you are not working or your role is being made redundant, consider how much financial pressure are you under and make sure you solve that issue first.

If you receive a healthy severance or redundancy package, remember that an extended period without work will eat into these savings, even though you may want a holiday or some time out. I can almost guarantee that if you are in a relationship, your partner will kick you under the table much sooner than you think to start bringing in an income again.

If you need to take a lower-paid job for a few months while you are looking, then do so. You do not need to state this on your resume or LinkedIn profile. As jobs today carry far less security than they used to, people are far more likely to understand that you need to support your family and yourself. If anyone asks, just say: "My role was made redundant and I decided to take a break".

It is far worse to sit back and turn down job offers because your ego is getting in the way of paid work, than to feel the satisfaction of earning and paying your way. When I returned to Australia a few years ago, I took a casual job selling wine in some of the local organic wineries just to pay the bills. It helped that the wine industry was my passion from three decades ago and nearly became my career. It also gave me confidence to land the consulting roles that I eventually won which in turn helped me create my training company.

I have worked with 'C' suite executives who have taken contract roles while interviewing for a permanent job because the work itself did not risk their brand in the market. It is far better to be working and getting paid than hope for a role which may not eventuate for many reasons.

Regardless of what your job is, everyone is capable of freelancing or contract work. My advice is usually to take whatever work you can find based on your skills. You can even write on your LinkedIn profile that you are freelancing while looking for permanent work. There is no harm in that at all.

10.2 SHOULD I SIGN EXCLUSIVELY TO ONE RECRUITER?

It is unlikely you will be asked to sign up with only one recruitment business. This is not how recruiters work, though they may encourage you to let them know if you are working with anyone else for reasons discussed already:

- They get paid for placing you and get nothing if someone else does
- They have to manage the expectations of their own clients about who may accept an offer

The only time I have seen exclusivity is when you are 'contracting on demand'.

'Contracting on demand' is a new way of working coming out of the freelance economy. You work with third parties who contract you out to their clients. While contract recruiting is not new, in some industries 'on demand' contracting is becoming more commonplace for IT, technology, healthcare, construction, mining, law and accounting.

'On demand' simply means that the recruitment businesses, or in some cases the end service providers, will have an ongoing requirement from their clients to provide staff on a project basis. You may be engaged for any time from a day to a year. As this work often requires people at short notice, some of these businesses will ask you to sign with them exclusively and they do this for two reasons:

- To ensure they keep you out of a competitive market and only available to them.
- To manage staffing needs for their clients.

I suggest you carefully consider the commercial terms of your contract and see if it provides you with a minimum of guaranteed work. You know your own financial goals and what you need. They will not prevent you from working for yourself or contracting privately to other companies, but they may restrict you from working with their competitors. Check the contracts and have a detailed conversation about expectations and termination clauses before you sign. Talk to your accountants, financial advisers or even a lawyer.

When working in London in 2016, I was advising a global law firm, Allen & Overy, about their on demand contract lawyer business, Peerpoint. Many of their competitors demanded exclusivity whereas they did not. They had such a strong brand that they attracted the best talent and did not need to lock people in. It is up to you to decide whether you need to sign an exclusivity agreement. A little later, I was coaching a client on which type of 'on demand' business would suit them best and they ended up signing an exclusivity agreement. Two years on I received an email saying how grateful they were as it was the best career and life decision they had ever made.

You need to consider your own needs and your unique situation. The bottom line is to be aware of what you are getting yourself into and ask good questions. Get enough information to make an informed decision and also try to negotiate the outcome that works best for you.

10.3 HOW DO I KNOW IF MULTIPLE AGENCIES ARE ADVERTISING THE SAME ROLE AND WHICH ONE SHOULD I APPLY TO?

I could easily write a case study on this alone, as it happens every day on all recruitment platforms in all cities around the world. Let me explain the why and how and provide some suggestions and questions to ask.

Employers, both big and small, have recruitment panels and in many cases they are trying to save money by working with fewer recruiters on fewer roles.

These panels work with different tiers, e.g. Tier 1, Tier 2, Tier 3, etc. reflecting the partnerships between them. Tier 1 recruitment agencies get preferential treatment. If a recruitment firm is not on the panel, they cannot submit a candidate for a job, though we have already discussed plenty of examples, especially speculative applications that can circumvent these rules. In my head hunting business, we certainly developed relationships with businesses that hired from us but whose terms were too onerous to join their panel. They were happy for us to send them candidates as they trusted us.

You may find that more than one Tier 1 firm is appointed, so you can have multiple recruitment consultants advertising the same role for one business.

You may also find that the employer does not provide their permission to advertise their name as the role may be sensitive; again, the role is advertised correctly.

It is frustrating for a recruiter doing work for a client to have that goodwill undermined by another recruiter who has no relationship with the client but is playing the game and hoping to introduce a great candidate. See Case Study 1 about Cassie Stone and Toby the recruiter from TC Consultants for an example of this.

You may also find that another consultancy, who is not on the panel, is also advertising the role. Now it gets a little more complicated.

This leads to the questions:

- How does a recruitment business advertise a job that either does not exist or where they have no relationship with the employer?
- What are phantom jobs?
- Do all jobs advertised really exist?

Recruiters need to fill their database. For this reason, many go on fishing expeditions where they advertise vacancies which do not exist or are generic. Only some of these roles are real.

- If it is a fishing expedition, when you apply you will probably learn little about the role or be told it has been filled already. You may be told: "There are likely to be other similar roles on offer soon which you could be suitable for". In the meantime, if you want, they add you to their database. With GDPR (General Data Protection Regulation) in Europe and privacy laws now getting stronger across the globe, many countries require you to consent to having your data stored, but this does not always mean they request your consent.

- When a recruiter advertises the same job as another, properly appointed, recruiter, they are likely doing so in the hope that a good candidate applies and they can use that quality as leverage to get a foot in the door of the employer. They are working on the premise that an employer will not turn down a great candidate regardless of the source. You can see this in Case Study 1, about Big Law, Alltech and the recruiter Toby. Be wary of this type of situation as you can easily end up with your resume in the hands of a 'Toby'.

- As the former owner of a head hunting business, there were many times when we advertised generic roles for one reason: to attract high quality candidates. The roles were for real long-term clients who had constant needs for the same positions. Regardless of when the role was advertised, the client/employer was always in a hiring cycle. This comes back to asking good questions of the recruiter. Do not make too many assumptions.

Pro Tip: Finding out whether a recruiter is genuine

You can find out whether the recruiter you are talking to can genuinely help you by applying the RISCQ formula (Part 7 also covers this area):

- Research—gather information, look at their website, social media, LinkedIn profile, ask your network.
- Intuition—are there are any red flags and can you resolve them.
- Selection—are they the right fit for you?
- Control/Choices—how much control do you have about your resume, the application process, are you making informed choices?
- Questions—what questions am I not asking, do I have all the information I need? If not, then ask more.

Some of those questions can include:

- Are you retained by the employer?
- Do you work with them exclusively?
- Are you on their preferred supplier list?
- Have you worked with them before?
- What is the hiring process?
- Do you know why they are hiring?
- How well do you know the hiring team?
- Can you find out any more information?

The more 'No's you get to the above questions, the more likely they are not a close partner of the employer. You still cannot dismiss them as they could be working with a new client and therefore the recruiter does not yet have the trust of the employer. You need to dig a little deeper and see if the recruiter is transparent with you about their client relationship. Find out if they can get more information so you can work out if you want to work with this recruiter.

The bottom line is that the recruiter is paid to provide a service to the employer and indirectly to you, the candidate. It is in the recruiter's best interests to help you. However, the employer is not too concerned about the candidates who were not offered the role and quickly forgets most of them.

I realise that job seeking can be frustrating as there are many different angles and nuances to working with recruiters. However, it always goes back to:

- Asking the right questions
- Doing your research
- Asking your network
- Listening to your intuition

I want to share a personal example of seeing a job ad which was not quite what it seemed but where it worked out very well.

Many years ago, I was in London with my wife and young daughters, having just shut the doors, at considerable emotional and financial expense, to the technology company I had been building. I needed to find work. I saw an ad posted for the managing director of a recruitment business and applied. I heard nothing for two weeks. Then I got a call suggesting that I was not suitable for the role advertised, but asking if I would come in for a talk about something else more suited to me.

As the talk was with the well-known TV personality, UK based recruitment entrepreneur and stalwart of the Dragon's Den, James Caan, I was intrigued. It turned out that the job ad he had placed had a twin purpose: first, to find someone to run one of his existing recruitment businesses and, second, to find someone to head up a new business venture. The second option was entirely speculative, although he did want to hire someone. James rolled out the red carpet. He entertained my wife and me with dinner at the Natural History Museum in London, underneath the dinosaurs, hosted by Prince Charles. It certainly left a positive and lasting impression. Three months later we signed the deal to work together, but fate took me back to Australia.

That speculative job ad carried the right intention and resulted in an offer. Remember to ask the right questions and see whether you want to pursue it. There is no point in getting frustrated with the process.

10.4 HOW DO I ADDRESS SELECTION CRITERIA IN A JOB AD?

In summary, I advise jobseekers to stick to the 70:30 rule. If you meet 70% of the selection criteria, then apply. Rarely does any candidate meet all the requirements. However, if the 30% you do not meet is all in the category of 'must haves' then you are unlikely to be successful. Read Chapter 6.7 for more detailed guidance around this.

The same rule goes for applying via recruiters; even the best recruiters cannot guarantee that sending your resume to the client will land you an interview. There are a few exceptions to this and I have worked on global hiring projects where every candidate we introduced to the potential employer was interviewed. Your recruiter will let you know your chances.

The 70% represents that you are good enough to hire. The other 30% is based on the knowledge that hiring requirements can be fluid. Employers will assess whether you can do the job, whether you will fit in culturally and whether you really want to work for them rather than take any job offered. Your resume may be good enough on paper, but your performance at interview and their hiring needs, salary, culture and fit will determine whether they make an offer. This comes down to your relevance and suitability for the role.

10.5 DO I NEED TO WRITE A COVER LETTER?

In short, for applications directly to employers, the answer is yes, always, unless the job ad specifically excludes it. You do not need to send a cover letter to submit your resume to, or work with, a recruiter. Read Part 6 for further details.

As you know, I have been an employer for most of my working life and across multiple industries around the world. I am always most impressed by those who send me a well-written and specific cover letter addressing three crucial points:

- What you know about my company
- Why you want to work here
- What value and benefit you bring to my company, including the difference you believe you can make.

Make sure you tailor the cover letter to each application. Unlike your resume, the cover letter is your opportunity to promote yourself in a personal and unique way. If you read it back and you think someone else could write the same letter, then it is neither unique nor specific.

The last point to note is that with technology and applicant tracking systems, an automated system is likely to filter your resume which may not be read by a human until a later stage of the process. However, your cover letter could differentiate you from the crowd and be a talking point for the interview.

10.6 WHAT INFORMATION SHOULD I DISCLOSE IF I HAVE HAD MEDICAL PROBLEMS?

My advice has always been the same: unless you have a current illness or disability that directly impacts your ability to execute the job you are applying for, there is nothing that you need to disclose.

As a cancer survivor, I have never needed to disclose my former illness. If I was required to undergo a medical, then it would no doubt be raised but take comfort in the knowledge that I have worked with many people who have had life-threatening and chronic conditions. To date none have been refused an offer because of it.

I will provide a general caveat here and suggest that the laws of your country and those of your employer will also determine how you are further protected. For example, if a US company employs you in London, then you may get protection from both countries. You need to check. The onus is on you.

10.7 HOW DO I ANSWER THE WEAKNESS QUESTION?

One of the most frequently asked questions, and one of the most challenging, is the question: "What are your weaknesses?"

It is best answered with the formula below:

- start with a strength
- sandwich the weakness in the middle
- end with a strength

Two example responses follow, but remember that employers expect us to have weaknesses and that the best employees show self-awareness and a willingness to learn.

For the perfectionist:

"I take a lot of pride in my work and can be a perfectionist, ensuring there are no mistakes with any projects I work on. This means that sometimes I put in extra hours to complete my work so I've learned to communicate better with my colleagues, ask for help and make sure that we all apply the same standards and I delegate where necessary."

The strength is that you take pride in your work. The weakness is that you work longer than others to get the job done which could impact your family life and overtime pay. The final strength is that you have learned to communicate better and ask for help from colleagues.

For the advisor and problem solver:

"I enjoy helping my colleagues and teams solve problems and I am often a sounding board for them. As a result, I often have more work to do than time to do it and dislike saying no to colleagues when they ask for help. So I've learned to prioritise tasks and inform colleagues when I can help and how long it will take to answer their questions in order of urgency. This means that more often they will first try to solve problems themselves."

The strength is your problem solving ability and that you are approachable. Your weakness is taking on too much work by not being able to say no. Your final strength is you learned to delegate and prioritise tasks (as well as empowering your colleagues to be more self-sufficient).

10.8 HOW DO I ANSWER THE SALARY QUESTION AND NEGOTIATE AN OFFER?

As a proactive job seeker, your current salary has little to do with what you will earn in your next role. This is because every employer has their own views and benchmark standards for pay and benefits. Your new employer may pay less but give more holidays, pensions/superannuation/401k, medical insurance, child care, parental leave and have better career opportunities. You need to weigh these up.

A few different scenarios can arise:

- When you have been head hunted
- When you are working
- When you are not working
- When you select a salary band during an online application

While you may be able to negotiate salary and conditions in most cases, there will be occasions when the salary is fixed, for example, with short-term contracts and fixed casual labour.

When you have been head hunted

The recruiter will ask about your financial requirements and aspirations in the initial conversations to make sure their client can meet your expectations. If your current package is well below their benchmarks, they may question your capability and experience, but either way they will ask. The really good recruiters know that some employers pay more than others and do not hold that against you.

This also allows you to decide whether you want to proceed with applying through them for the job.

I recommend being as honest as possible and negotiate when you get an offer. The recruiters will tell you what is realistic and are often better at negotiating than you. They are experts at it and their commission may depend upon it. Recruiters are also a great source of salary information and guides. Make the most of their expertise and knowledge.

When you are working

When you are looking to move jobs by applying directly to employers, they can ask you the salary question at any stage of the interview process, including the initial pre-screening call.

Usually, discussing money and benefits is best left until the offer stage. By then you know how badly you want to work for them and how much you are prepared to compromise. You can try to negotiate on pretty much anything in the offer letter; notice periods, holidays, probationary periods, bonuses, pay and benefits. Know your strengths and what they need from you and use that as leverage for your negotiations. You want to be reasonable, not the candidate that the employer realises will be difficult when they start. Find that balance and come from a place of strength.

There are four ways you can respond to the salary question:

- I prefer to find out more about the role first and we can discuss salary and benefits at a later stage.
- I saw the role was advertised for between X and Y. I would prefer to be at Y. Please tell me what determines whether it is at the lower or higher end of the band.
- I am looking for a competitive market package.
- I understand that the market rate is X. Please can you tell me what you are offering?

When you are not working

The same principles and answers above apply here; you are aiming for market rate for that industry and that employer. My advice is to understand what your financial needs are. What is the minimum you need to earn to support yourself and your family? Make sure you get that. You should not disclose your minimum but keep it in the back of your mind when negotiating. If that number is well below what they are offering, then you are fine. If it is close, make sure you really sell your strengths, your features and how they benefit the employer. Then work out what is more important; pay, benefits, or flexibility with child care.

The point is to make sure you have a firm base to negotiate from to secure the job. If the role pays less than you want, then maybe you can negotiate a review within a certain timeframe, for example, at the end of a probation period or within 3 months, 6 months or 12 months. This negotiation will almost always be based on your performance once you start, so ensure you negotiate metrics which you can hit. If possible, confirm this in writing either in the contract or by separate email.

I have coached many high earning 'C' suite executives who have sensibly taken less well paid roles on a contract basis while looking for permanent work. *Some are able to use that experience as leverage when negotiating a full-time role. In addition, it provides:*

- Continued confidence and exposure to new products and methods while employed
- A salary to support their family
- An opportunity to negotiate an extension or convert it to a permanent role if the external job market is weak when their contract comes to an end.

The biggest lesson we can all learn when not working is not to be precious about our corporate or professional identity. Remove ego from the job search about what we used to earn and what we used to do. It no longer matters. I have had to apply it to myself before. It was initially a painful lesson, but I said to myself every day: "I am excited and grateful to have this opportunity". Changing and reframing the language that we use helps to create and maintain a positive mindset which we take with us and into our work.

Online applications

When you apply directly to an employer or fill out a form on a recruiter's website, they often ask you to select a salary band. ***Carry out some research to find out the market rate:***

- Ask recruiters for their salary guides
- Do a Google search for salary guides for similar roles
- Find similar jobs which advertise salaries and then work out what your financial needs are
- Take into account your current or previous salary if in a similar role and aim for the highest band within your market rate

They will often try to negotiate you down from your position, but it is far harder for you to negotiate up when you have already told them what you want to be paid.

Remember that these are also just guides and are not necessarily reflective of what you will earn.

Negotiation Case Study

The following short case study on negotiating salary and benefits highlights many of the areas above, especially when your role may have been made redundant or you are in career transition. It shows that it does not matter what your previous role was and what you earned.

I was coaching a friend whose entire division of his investment bank had been shut down. He was the global head and had been with the bank since graduating nearly 25 years before. For such a senior executive, at a time when the banking industry was suffering from scrutiny and a weak economy, he found that positions he wanted were in short supply. However, he had built a considerable network and received an offer from a much smaller brokerage before he had finished closing down the unit.

I remember the conversation well. He was grateful for the offer but felt that he been low balled financially. He was not very enthusiastic. Sitting in his garden in London after a wonderful Sunday lunch with our children running around, we were able to talk sensibly. His concern was that he had been used to earning a certain amount and felt they would use all of his skills and knowledge but not pay his market rate because of his situation. In addition, the scope of the role was more limited. He liked the company but was demotivated by their offer.

I suggested he renegotiate his offer around his expertise and how they would use it, having measurable benchmarks for salary and performance review. If it was a lesser role, then it would be stress-free and he could spend more time with his family with less work pressure. After a long corporate career, he could see this as a healthy break. Their position was that he was being hired because of all his expertise. However, they did not need it for this role, though they would lean on him occasionally for additional support, so they did not need to pay an executive package. In essence, they were offering him a role with less responsibility and lower pay. There are many people I know who, after a long and stressful senior management career, opt for a position with less responsibility to enjoy and often rebuild their family life. This was not the case. His suspicion was that as soon as he joined, they would give him all the work his expertise reflected, but not the job title or money.

His negotiating request was to review his role six months and twelve months after he started. If he had carried out agreed prescribed tasks and activities, including foreign travel, new client relationships, increasing client revenue, and management of local and international teams, his role would be formally recognised and his remuneration would increase to agreed levels. This way his employer knew that if they wanted to use the full scope of his expertise, they would have to compensate him fairly, which was calling their bluff. He would either go home stress-free at the end of each day in a reduced role or be compensated for being a part of their executive. He negotiated and accepted their offer.

PART 11:
SECURING YOUR FUTURE

11.1 WORK IS NOT LIFE.

Thank you for joining me this far. I have a few final tips I would like to share with you about your career journey.

Work is different for all of us and your unique job search will serve a different purpose at each stage of your life. I have no doubt you have read much about finding your passion and purpose in life, and that when you align it to your work, you will be fulfilled. There is certainly a huge amount of merit in that, but I personally believe there is one step further: your mission. One thing I know for certain is that while our life's purpose remains the same, I also know that our passions and interests change through life along with the way we express ourselves.

Don't get too caught up in this. I see many people lose a sense of identity, value and direction because they are looking backwards to what they have done and their previous identity rather than focusing on what life experience, knowledge and technical skills can help them going forwards.

Your own mission may be a short-term plan to take contracting work to fund travel for the next few years. It could be taking a high-powered executive job as leverage for the next stage of your career, or it could be taking a lower paid role to de-stress while you work out what you really want to do in life. Having advised tens of thousands of people, I know that those of you with a clear mission tend to be happier. Sometimes, not always, it explains why, in a toxic work environment, some cope far better than others; because they have a plan.

What are your values, strengths, skills, desires, passion and dreams? What do you need to learn? What do you like to do? How important are these to you? Spend time reflecting. Then go and learn what you need to or find a job and employer that invests in you.

If I look at my own career, I practiced law as a barrister, a lawyer, in London then became a head hunter before setting up a recruitment business in Australia and India. After selling my business, I became a technology start-up founder, then set up a women's and girls' wear fashion business with my wife. I learned new skills and methodologies and applied the knowledge that I accumulated along the way. Now I combine all of those skills to build and run a career training and life strategy company.

Your work does not define you and your qualifications need not dictate your career journey. I have not practiced law for 25 years, but I still use that knowledge and discipline every week. My identity is not governed by that qualification. Life and work are never linear and it is entirely up to you how you craft your career and how you choose to live your life.

I know there will be some of you who believe your career as a designer, doctor, lawyer, accountant, even banker will define your life and that you have studied so hard to be that person and have that identity. But many professions, and it does not matter what you studied, are changing. For some of you, they do not serve you any more or enable you to thrive. For a few of you whose parents have paid for your education and steered you down those paths, there will be disappointment and, in some cases, outrage but remember that they have had their chance at life and now this is yours. If you choose to leave your current career, remember that all the knowledge and expertise you have gained, both technically and in life as a human, will stay with you. I have worked with many people in career transition who forget they have incredible talents because it has not been highlighted or overtly valued. For every one of you looking to leave a corporate career and embark on a new journey into the world of freelance work, the gig economy or building a side business to create an entrepreneurial life, there will also be someone who loves their corporate salaried or professional life. Not everyone wants to run their own business or be a consultant. I have great friends, who I have huge respect and admiration for, who, having owned successful businesses, have decided never to do so again. The factor they all have in common is a mission; they know the journey they are on and their creative passion and interests are met with what they do away from their everyday job. They enjoy their work but their individual mission is clear; they have a goal and sometimes many goals.

Work is part of your life but your friends love you because of who you are, what you stand for and what you contribute unconditionally to them. They don't care what you do for a job. They can respect and admire your work, but the work does not define your relationship with them. I say this because I coach so many people both young and older who have become so connected to their identity at work that they have lost their connection to their values. In most cases, when their career ends or a redundancy takes place, that illusion of identity is shattered and they are lost.

I recommend you craft a career and work that supports you in every aspect of life, that allows you to dive deep into your friendships, family, interests and passions and that you do this to support yourself equally emotionally, physically, mentally and spiritually. Find and build a mission to support and sustain this. You deserve it. It is your birthright to be fulfilled in all elements of life. Do not give those choices away to anyone. Yes, we all suffer crises in life, but the more resilience and self-awareness we have built into our life as a whole, the better equipped we are for life's trials and uncertainties.

I wish you all the very best with your job search and life.

Make good choices and ask good questions.

Be kind to yourself and others.

With love and gratitude.

Thank you.

ACKNOWLEDGEMENTS

This journey started off as a simple quest to share my knowledge of the job search process and how to manage working with recruiters. This book became so much more and I have a new found respect for authors, graphic designers, editors, typesetters and all of the wonderful people who helped turn my thoughts into an actionable guide.

As mentioned at the beginning thank you to Loren Trlin for sewing the idea that knowledge is wasted unless shared.

My editor Rananda Rich, or as she is known the Inkrat, has been incredible. She steered me through the process of a first time author with grace, direction and kindness where at times I have been immensely challenged and frustrated. This book is a reflection on her ability to transform thoughts and scribbles into a book.

Melinda Ly is a very talented designer and she has transformed my title into a visual masterpiece and cover. She has taken me through the design process explaining form, colour, shape and emotion. Thank you.

I would also like to mention Tucker Max and JT McCormick of Scribe Media. JT is a guest on my podcast Human Impact and his thoughts resonate with me today. Although I did not use Scribe formally for this project I have digested Tucker's book on self-publishing and all of his wisdom.

For my wife, Dimity and daughters Viva and Isla. They have been patient and tolerant when I have been consumed in writing and less present than I should have been. I love you.

If you would like to contact me you will find me at www.edandrew.com

Thank You.

www.ingramcontent.com/pod-product-compliance
Lightning Source LLC
Chambersburg PA
CBHW022039190326
41520CB00008B/643